THE
AMAZON
ROADMAP

THE AMAZON ROADMAP

HOW INNOVATIVE BRANDS ARE REINVENTING THE PATH TO MARKET

BETSY MCGINN
AND
PHILIP SEGAL

The Amazon Roadmap: How Innovative Brands are Reinventing the Path to Market
By Betsy McGinn and Philip Segal
1. BUSINESS & ECONOMICS/E-Commerce/General
2. COMPUTERS/Electronic Commerce 3. BUSINESS & ECONOMICS/E-Commerce/Internet Marketing
Paperback ISBN: 978-1-949642-02-5
eBook ISBN: 978-1-949642-03-2

Cover design by Laura Duffy

Printed in the United States of America

Authority Publishing
11230 Gold Express Dr. #310-413
Gold River, CA 95670
800-877-1097
www.AuthorityPublishing.com

DEDICATION

Amazon has created an entirely new pathway for brands to enter the market. We are privileged to work with many of these innovative brands in the healthy consumables space. Our passions for digital technology and a healthier society—for both people and our environment—converge with our clients to work toward growing their businesses while bettering the planet.

We dedicate this book to that endeavor and to all the innovators fighting the good fight. We're grateful to be able to contribute to your efforts.

Big thanks to our talented editor, Madeleine Berenson, our invaluable road-side assistance.

And of course, to our beloveds—Phil's wife, Jessica, and children, Riley, Keira, and Charlie, and Betsy's husband, Brian—who always support and inspire us toward a better world for their sake and for all of humanity.

CONTENTS

FOREWORD

Poor Charles Darwin, he of the *HMS Beagle*, always gets misquoted. It is not survival of the *fittest* (i.e., the strongest, smartest, etc.) but of the most *adaptable*. Goodness knows that large consumer packaged goods (CPG) companies are well occupied by highly accomplished, intelligent, well-educated folks, but they have until recently been largely out of step in terms of where the consumer is going. Likewise, large conventional retailers have been struggling to remake themselves in a world where consumers are spoiled by Amazon, everyone has a smartphone, and people are not stopping to shop—they are shopping all the time.

To illustrate: while perhaps not universal, in the natural products space, there was a well-worn path to bringing products to market. Emerging brands followed a playbook of sorts. An entrepreneur with a great idea might venture out of their kitchen into farmers markets. From there, they would look to get their products into independent health food shops. The next big step was landing a beachhead customer like Whole Foods Market, Wegmans, or Sprouts, which would leverage them into a national distributor. This would give them access to hundreds or thousands of retailers. From there, the company would eventually migrate into supermarkets, mass accounts like Target and Walmart, perhaps Costco, and possibly some of the additional channels such as food service, chain drug, convenience, and more.

While this was the world we lived in, it required a lot of capital or long, hard years of bootstrapping to scale. There were expenses like slotting fees and free fills, ad programs with retailers and distributors, and promotional allowances of all kinds. One needed a sales team and brokers for each channel, and there was an ongoing everyday battle to get on the shelf, stay on the shelf, improve your shelf position, exceed hurdle rates, keep spending, and hope you made it through the next category review.

Well...that world has been turned upside down and tossed out the window.

There has been an explosion of business online through eCommerce and direct to consumer (DTC). Traditional brick-and-mortar retailers of all kinds are figuring out click and collect, home delivery, their own eCommerce, and even setting up unmanned pick up centers and integrating ordering through smart speakers at home.

To compound the vertigo for CPG marketers and traditional retailers, hard discounters like Aldi and Lidl have been on the rise. New channels like WeWork and meal kits such as Blue Apron and Sun Basket are siphoning off business from someone.

According to a study by the Food Marketing Institute (FMI) and A.C. Nielsen ("Digitally Engaged Food Shopper"), online grocery sales are expected to be $100 billion by 2022. The volume of groceries sold online in 2017 was equal to about 764 supermarkets; by 2025, that volume will be equivalent to 3,900 grocery stores. We can't simply watch the world go by—we must throw ourselves in and figure it out or be left behind.

Lord Baelish of *Game of Thrones* famously intoned, "Chaos is a ladder." In this case, I heartily concur. The remarkable growth of Amazon, eCommerce in general, and DTC has created an abundance of opportunities for entrepreneurs and CPG companies to reach consumers. In all this hurly burly, there has never been a more fertile and amazing time to launch a brand, have access to capital, and make your own success. Those who embrace this change and recognize it as the new normal are *adapting* to this reality and are meeting the consumer where they want to engage with their brand.

To be an entrepreneur, brand owner, or marketer today, you need be literate in the ways of eCommerce, DTC, and—it's so big as to block out the sun—Amazon.

But one does not simply walk into Mordor. Thankfully... graciously, Betsy McGinn and Phil Segal have shared so much of their expertise and hard-won experience in an incredibly thoughtful and organized way in this fine publication. This book walks you through how to get started in eCommerce (and notably, Amazon) and provides a comprehensive but accessible understanding of how to not only succeed, but more importantly, how to integrate these initiatives with the rest of your omnichannel activities to achieve your strategic and business objectives. In fact, for many companies, online is becoming their launchpad into brick-and-mortar. Brands are taking their learnings, their validation of consumer acceptance, and even their reviews and data on how many consumers they have in a retailer's trading area to make their case to get onto store shelves.

Whether you are a founder navigating your way through the constant chop, a manager responsible for delivering results, or a senior executive seeking to understand the big picture, this book is a *gift*.

It will dramatically accelerate your climb up the learning curve of this new reality and help you win by arming you with the knowledge and lessons that you can bring and apply to your business.

By the time you are through, you will…

- Understand that an eCommerce strategy is essential to your business.
- Understand the changing landscape.
- Appreciate the strategic considerations around product configuration, pricing, freight implications, and effective marketing programs.
- Understand how to execute internally and outsource resources.

You will develop your new playbook. Good luck and success in your travels.

Bob Burke, Natural Products Consulting, LLC

Bob has been a consultant for 21 years, helping companies bring natural, organic, and specialty products to market. He is coauthor of the Natural Products Field Manual, *produces sales and financing seminars, serves on boards and advisory boards, and prior to consulting led sales at Stonyfield Farm. He was named as one of the top 25 business builders over the last 25 years by* Natural Foods Merchandiser *magazine. Please see NaturalConsulting.com.*

INTRODUCTION

Amazon has quite the reputation as a business killer. CEO Jeff Bezos's genius is rivaled only by his ruthless competitiveness. He once famously said, "*Your* margin is *my* opportunity," and he follows that playbook to the letter. But we believe the whole story is more complex.

Is Amazon a formidable threat to brands and retailers whose undifferentiated goods offer little additional value to the consumer? Yes. Is it an entirely new business model that challenges the internal capabilities of many traditional consumer products companies? Yes again. So if you have a commoditized product or a weak brand, or you are a company that can't shift from traditional ways of thinking and doing business, you definitely should be worried about the way Amazon has changed the marketplace. (And that goes double if you can be replaced by a white-label alternative!)

But while Amazon is ringing the death knell for entrenched retailers with questionable added value, it's an extraordinarily powerful launch pad for new and innovative brands. There is no other platform with Amazon's scale, reach, and buying intent, not to mention unmatched fulfillment capabilities. So if your product is well formulated, meets a market need, and is well received by your audience, Amazon is probably the best, cheapest, and most scalable platform to grow your business. And it can be an exciting ride for your brand.

But there's good excitement and bad excitement. And being prepared before you start this undertaking can help ensure the good kind and minimize the bad. You'd be surprised by the number of people who don't invest in that preparation. While it may seem obvious that you have to be retail-ready before you attempt retail execution, way too many brands jump online before they've done their homework.

You wouldn't think of driving across the country without making sure your car is tuned up and in good functioning shape, maybe even do a little clean-up and get rid of those gum wrappers under the seat. And those are just the basics. The best road trips start with a well-researched and thought-out travel plan based on expert sources—maps, GPS, and travel guides that tell you where the good campgrounds, hotels, restaurants, and off-the-beaten-path sightseeing spots are. These experts also help you anticipate and plan for trouble spots. Will you need snow tires if you're driving through the Rocky Mountains in February? Knowing likely scenarios not only makes the trip more enjoyable for everyone involved, it also gives you confidence and flexibility, so you can adapt without losing focus when things don't go your way.

So think of the act of taking your business to Amazon as a road trip for your company. Sure, you could just get in your car and go, deal with the oil leak when it happens, and just *hope* it doesn't happen on US 50…in Nevada…at midnight. You could just list your products and hope they fly off the virtual shelf. But why take those risks, especially if there's a proven low chance of success when you do?

The fact is, the most successful brands on Amazon did extraordinary advance work before they even arrived at Amazon's door. They sought knowledge, developed a strategy, and executed meticulously. They understood that it takes months of patiently tweaking and refining tactics to get Amazon's flywheel moving and their sales soaring.

Now more than ever, there's an especially big opportunity in the grocery universe, because Amazon is making eCommerce (henceforth known as eComm) a reality in the world of grocery. Along with the general quest to provide ever-faster distribution and shipping, Amazon is working to infiltrate the most regular consumer household categories, with offerings like Fresh, Prime Now, and Prime Pantry. Their completely unexpected 2017 acquisition of Whole Foods Market cemented their commitment to this trajectory and sent shock waves through Wall Street, with the stock prices of competing retailers like Kroger, Costco, and Sprouts dropping 5%–10% overnight.

That initial reaction was a bit overblown. Much has changed since the acquisition, but the announcement that rocked us all didn't exactly end the grocery world as we know it. (Later in the book, we share an interview with a Whole Foods Market expert.) But we are as aware as anyone of how much and how quickly Amazon will continue to change and evolve. That's why, like Bezos, we believe it's all about the long game.

The goal of this book is to provide a basis of knowledge and understanding that you can use as a foundation for your strategy and success. We focus on the core elements that make Amazon unique compared to other platforms and selling channels, and the work you need to do as a brand to succeed. So even though the specific tactics will change over time, this basic framework should remain largely intact.

Think of it as our roadmap for your Amazon journey, one that describes what it will look like, based on our extensive experience in the industry with countless brands. Together, we've worked with Amazon a total of 16 years, and through all the changes we've witnessed, one truth has remained the same: preparation is key. We think the opportunity that Amazon affords new and innovative companies who previously didn't stand a chance of making it to a retail shelf is incredibly exciting, and we absolutely love having a hand in building the foundation for their success.

Here's to the good kind of excitement that comes with a vision, a plan, preparation, and finally…success!

PLAN

1

❦

DOROTHY, YOU'RE NOT IN BRICK & MORTAR ANYMORE!

Ecommerce is different.

And we don't mean in the obvious way of walking into a store versus shopping online at home in your pajamas. We mean that along with a new mode of selling comes a whole new way of thinking about your brand and doing business.

In recent years, an untold number of new companies have launched their brands online, bypassing the traditional path to the grocery store shelf, and making a market entry where they largely control their own destiny. The shelves may come later, but many new and smaller companies, known as "micro-brands" (or affectionately as "ankle biters" by their big CPG competitors) are getting ahead online before they even consider approaching a major retailer.

Why is that? Well, some of the differences between the retail store model and eComm are daunting to larger CPGs. That stands in the way of taking a leap of faith into the channel that's clearly the growth driver in retail sales. The biggest hurdle for many large companies is the need for certainty of success—no leaps of faith here. Our clients often ask how large the category is and what they can expect their share to be. The irrelevance of this question cannot be overstated: the size of your category online today will be different tomorrow, no matter what size it is. No category is mature, and as eComm continues to drive retail growth, every category continues to expand.

So answering the question "What can I expect my share to be?" is nearly impossible. Your level of success is largely up to you. There are major CPG brands with a small or even nonexistent share of their category online, because it was captured instead by brands who seized the early opportunity in eComm, and Amazon in particular. KIND Bar and Seventh Generation are two notable examples of brands that entered the Amazon ecosystem early and flourished as a result. So your share is linked to the effort you expend, in a world that offers a vast array of tools to grow your business inside and outside of Amazon.

This uncertainty with the online sales model creates a risk that a lot of large CPGs haven't yet overcome. Reports that identify clear opportunity—like Nielsen and SPINS do in brick-and-mortar—are virtually nonexistent online. And this isn't a coincidence. Amazon set the standard early by keeping retail sales data close to the vest. Other e-tailers have followed suit, and why shouldn't they? There's hardly any upside for Thrive Market or Jet.com to provide public reporting transparency, and without any certainty about share of market, potential volume, or how competitors are faring, many large CPG companies are cautiously sticking their toes in the water at best and are immobilized at worst.

For a long time, eComm flew under the radar of brick-and-mortar retailers and even most major brands. At first, some considered these sales opportunities incremental and inconsequential to their thriving retail store business. But now, with thousands of stores closing each year, the direction of retail shopping is what's unclear. And while some brands have been standing on the sidelines waiting for data to definitively illuminate the size of the prize, others are racing ahead with this new retail opportunity.

WHAT MAJOR DIFFERENCES DEFINE THE SPACE?

First, relationships. They're not as important.

It sounds antithetical to a successful business to dismiss the significance of relationships, but at Amazon, they take a back seat to automation. Traditionally, retail buyers were the gatekeepers to product placement, which is the reason major brands had the ability to shut out the vast array of smaller ones. Traditional brands still expect relationships to be key to their online success. But embracing automation gets you further.

Amazon has created a brand new "equi-system," where companies of all sizes can play and win. For the most part, they've taken humans out of the equation, and that's what makes Amazon such a trusted platform for consumers. In fact, for several consecutive years, the Boston-based Reputation Institute has ranked (RepTrak, 2018) Amazon as either the first or second most reputable company in the US.

At Amazon, humans don't decide which products get on the shelf, how they'll be priced, or who gets priority in promotional opportunities. Truth is, if you're hinging your Amazon success on a relationship with a human, you'll be waiting for a very long time. Vendor Managers at Amazon oversee huge categories with thousands of brands, and reserve the human touch for brands selling millions of dollars of product on the platform. That's a high threshold, so human intervention isn't as relevant to a brand's success. Amazon increasingly automates all aspects of its transactions, which is good news for brands that are willing to accept the challenge of doing business differently. So Rule #1: automation is your friend. Brands that embrace this concept win. Brands that don't? They struggle.

In traditional retail, while large brands can afford to "pay to play," the cost of slotting is beyond the reach of many small and medium-size brands. But at Amazon, there's no slotting. There are other costs of doing business, of course, but those are linked directly to sales, so they don't require an extraordinary up-front investment, a potential total loss to a brand that doesn't prove its worth on the retail shelf within the required trial period.

Speaking of trial periods, the next big difference between stores and eComm is this: In stores, after you pay slotting for your place on the shelf, you have a limited amount of time—usually three to six months—to meet a set threshold of sales. And if you don't, you're out. But Amazon, with its unlimited "shelf space," values variety over velocity. (After all, they are The Everything Store.) With over 400 fulfillment centers nationwide, there's plenty of room for bestsellers *and* all of the long-tail items consumers have a hard time finding anywhere else. We've seen some of the most underrated items in a company's portfolio become bestsellers on Amazon, solely because of this new bridge to the consumer.

This doesn't mean that Amazon doesn't have standards for success. On the contrary, the company sets a high bar for other strategic factors like product quality, ample shelf life, product availability, and most importantly, positive consumer experience. In fact, consumer experience is where Amazon does put an emphasis on relationships—and what an emphasis it is! If you have a terrific body lotion that people love but it leaks all over the potato chips and cashmere sweater in the shipping box, your listing will be shut down in a flash. And now, the burden is on you to not only fix the issue but also to *convince* Amazon that you have. Bottom line: "no slotting" means room for everyone at the door, but you have to hold up your end of Amazon's commitment to create stellar consumer experiences.

Here's another difference that may surprise you. Those strategic retail store price points of $3.99 and $4.99? They're mostly meaningless on Amazon, for two reasons. First, consumers typically purchase in multipacks on Amazon, which don't readily display these standard retail price points. And second, pricing in general is all over the map.

We've seen products with double their brick-and-mortar retail price rise to top sellers on Amazon. We've also seen brands with the lowest price point on Amazon not only drive themselves into unprofitability, but also negatively impact their brick-and-mortar retail channels. And nothing will ruin your business in the rest of the market faster than a low price on Amazon that infuriates your retail partners. We'll expand on this in Chapter 6, but for now, know that Amazon customers, like all customers, want a fair price, but they also value selection, convenience, and—in the case of over 100 million Prime members—free two-day shipping.

Another thing that catches a lot of brands by surprise is that trade rates and general costs of doing business may be very different than the existing sales and operations model. And we hear both extremes—that Amazon is exceptionally profitable for some brands but not so much for others. Trade rates are high, typically higher than other retail channels, but other costs of doing business can be lower than these same channels. It's crucial to thoroughly understand all of these inputs before selling a single product on Amazon (a topic also addressed in Chapter 6). But again, for now, know that the business is more complex than it seems and that to have a successful Amazon business, it's essential to know every variable that impacts your profitability.

Finally, promotional strategy is an entirely new paradigm online. In brick-and-mortar, effective promotions usually follow a high/low price promotion strategy. The tried-and-true promotional formula is a discount program once per quarter, accompanied by an ad placement or display. But online, the goal is discoverability and conversion, which requires an "always on" strategy. Your product is the needle in a haystack on Amazon, and unless you actively guide consumers to it specifically, they'll either buy the needle in the haystack they come across first or the one they know where to find.

Online, bringing eyeballs to your brand is a constant must; helping potential customers discover your brand, converting them from the brand they used to buy, and keeping them loyal to yours is what leads you to success. Too many people think that if they get their brand listed on Amazon, it will be an instant overnight success. But without an investment in key online marketing tools, they're setting themselves up for disappointment. (More about this in Chapter 7.)

These basic differences between eComm and brick-and-mortar illustrate some of the attitudinal and structural shifts your company has to make to optimize your success on Amazon. But any company with both

Amazon and retail presence will tell you that the complete list of differences is much longer. They'll also tell you that committing to this change is so worth it! Where else can you take your product to an unlimited shelf, one that offers instant national distribution without slotting and provides you with control over your marketing activities? (And an added bonus for all of us introverts: we don't have to interact with a live person!)

New landscapes always require some kind of adjustment, but we're confident this eComm evolution will become less painful over time. After all, when Costco came onto the scene, very few CPG companies believed in their business model or expected they'd be around for long. Brands resisted working on tighter margins, developing unique packs, or even considering a business that would in some cases offer only in-and-out placement opportunities.

Now, not only have we all adapted to this model, but it's also been integrated into the DNA of the consumer products industry. Even small and regional brands are able to take advantage of the life-changing opportunity that Costco offers. So think of Amazon as the new Costco—a business model to be embraced and honed as a whole new opportunity for your company and your brand.

THE NEW DNA OF RETAIL

While being diagnosed with lupus was not the only life-changing moment for CEO Amy Lacey, it was the catalyst for many to come. Cali'flour Foods, the wildly successful cauliflower pizza crust company she cofounded, was conceived in response to this health threat. Every Friday night, Amy and her family would have Family Fun Night, which included games and pizza. Every Saturday morning she would wake with severe arthritis pain. As a result, Amy was looking online for grain-free and gluten-free pizza crust recipes and started experimenting with cauliflower, a vegetable that is easy to work with, because it takes on the flavors of whatever you make. She came up with her own recipe, and together with her daughter and a fellow health coach, she found a way to make a consistent product.

As a life and health coach at that time, Amy would serve her newly created pizza to clients at happy hour and, most importantly, to her family on Family Fun Night. Even her non-vegetable-eating son loved it. Next, she took it to the farmers market, where the line of fans to buy her cauliflower pizza crusts went up the street. A company was born.

She decided to launch first through eComm on her own website in March 2016, and by December, she was selling on Amazon. One thing we really wanted to hear from Amy is how they solved the issue of selling and shipping a perishable product, a prospect that daunts most other perishable brands.

Shipping was not easy and, in the early days, there were many all-nighters at the Cali'flour warehouse to get packages out the door. Amy told us how they tried to optimize their direct-shipping model. "We used a specific insulated kangaroo shipping envelope with no-sweat ice packs. We calculated the shipping costs based on our own testing. But what we didn't realize was that when these packs get into certain temperatures, they expand, which changes the UPS rates based on dimensional weight. When we got the shipping bill, it was ten times more than we expected." An expensive mistake and a great motivator to find a solution.

Through great networking and asking the right questions, Amy was able to work with packaging specialists for a home-delivery meal kit company (the folks who know how to deliver a piece of fish to your front porch and keep it fresh until you arrive home from work). However, since her pizza crusts are fully baked, she was able to tweak her packaging to provide a great customer experience while also reining in fulfillment costs.

They carefully determined which products to sell on their own site and which to offer specifically to Amazon, "treating Amazon like its own unique platform." But the question remained: would Amazon consumers buy the product and pay for shipping? After thoughtful testing, they determined that consumers are more willing to buy a product at a premium retail price that includes shipping than the same product at a lower price with shipping tacked on. "With growth being what it is, we can also now afford to take a little hit on margin to give that free shipping."

When we asked Amy for advice for other perishable brands, she said this:

"Be sure to do your homework. Shop around for fulfillment options. We found that costs vary widely and can be as low as $2 or as high as $10 per package. Also, network—talk to people and ask questions."

All of this hard work has enabled Cali'flour to self-fund their business and grow to a point where they are being invited into retail. Amy credits her company's success to being part of a new uncrowded category, but it's important to note that as a new or small brand, it's often hard to develop a new category because of the investment needed to get the brand—and sometimes even the category itself—on the map.

"The beautiful thing about Amazon is that you are able to dictate your outcomes. Now we have the money to move forward in grocery, and do it with a bang."

2

——⟨⊘/⊘⟩——

THE THREE RULES OF AMAZON SUCCESS: QUALITY, QUALITY, & QUALITY

We could tell you that on Amazon, good marketing will make up for a bad product, but we'd be lying.

Yes, there are examples of businesses that have managed to build massive sales with mediocre or even subpar products in other retail channels, but this doesn't fly on Amazon. Even if there's some initial success, a bad product on Amazon eventually either declines in sales velocity or fails altogether.

Why, you ask? Because, as any Amazon rep will tell you, if you strip away the buying functionality from Amazon. com, you're left with "the world's largest recommendation engine."

And *that* is true.

Product discovery algorithms and useful, detailed, and authentic customer reviews have been distinguishing advantages of Amazon's since the beginning. *Then* they launched the unrivaled product selection, mind-boggling fulfillment capabilities, cloud computing services, and countless other business lines.

So while you may be able to drive sales velocity with any number of marketing tactics, if your product is not well received by purchasers, they *will* make their way back to Amazon to share their experience, often with explicitness and vehemence.

For better or worse, there is nowhere to hide from the court of public opinion on Amazon. And the feedback record is prominently featured for all to see. In fact, many prospective customers come to Amazon *just* to read product reviews when they're buying offline or from another website. Then they often end up either buying from Amazon or not buying at all, depending on what they find!

Here is your roadmap for success:

DETERMINE A MARKET NEED

There are basically two strategies for selling your product:

1. Meet existing demand.
2. Create demand via marketing.

Creating demand generally requires a huge marketing budget, spent strategically over time. That's not achievable for most businesses, especially start-ups. Yes, there are examples of incredibly cheap marketing campaigns that went viral and propelled the business to overnight success, but people also win the lottery. In other words, they're unicorn stories that can't be predictably repeated.

So we're left with the first strategy: creating a product that effectively satisfies an existing consumer demand. Hopefully, you believe your product does this. But definitively validating demand before overcommitting resources to development is easier said than done. Luckily for modern entrepreneurs, the internet provides fabulous tools that just weren't available before.

DETERMINE VOLUME FOR RELEVANT SEARCH TERMS

Knowing the number of searches for a certain word or phrase can provide some immediate, relatively accurate data to not only validate but also maybe even quantify your market size. People use search engines every day to ask questions and look for products and services; search engines record this and trend it out over time. That data can be incredibly valuable to your business in the early and middle stages: from idea conception to validating a market to launching marketing campaigns.

Amazon doesn't share search-volume data for their platform, but Google has for a very long time, via their Keyword Tool. In most cases, this data can be used as a proxy for Amazon. Start with a general idea of how customers might search for your product, and from there, Google's tool can use these seed terms to extrapolate to even more relevant terms (but watch out for the less relevant ones sprinkled in), as well as quantify the average number of searches each month for these terms.

As of 2018, there's no official tool provided or recommended by Amazon, but there are some third-party tools that attempt to estimate search data on Amazon and allow you to search by keyword or product. Keyword search data is a unique, extremely valuable information source that reveals how consumers are searching for your products and in what proportions for each word or phrase. This type of data just isn't available in most other marketing or selling channels.

VALIDATE THE PRODUCT AND GAIN INITIAL TRACTION

There are countless stories of businesses that failed because either the product was a solution for a problem nobody had, they couldn't convince consumers that their product solved the problem, or the idea was just ahead of its time.

Ideally, you work to validate the market for your product (or product idea) in some way before committing to full development. You can do this through a survey, a simple landing page with some paid traffic from Google or Facebook, a crowdfunding campaign, consumer panels, or even a soft launch with a small batch of product.

DEVELOP THE HIGHEST QUALITY PRODUCT POSSIBLE TO MEET THAT DEMAND

We're not product development experts, and we can't tell you *how* to create the highest quality product possible. But we can tell you with full confidence that it's a competitive world out there, new products are born and die every day, and the nearly universal accessibility that Amazon provides the consumer means they don't have to "settle" anymore. The bottom line: your product needs to be better than at least some, and maybe even all, of your competitors. And not just in your opinion, but according to third parties and customers, many of whom will be quite vocal with their opinions.

You can't please everyone, of course, and that shouldn't be the goal. But if you can't please *anyone at all*, the sooner you find that out, the better.

QUALITY AND INNOVATION WITH SOME TRADITION

Drew Westervelt, founder of HEX Performance, an innovative line of laundry and cleaning products, talked to us about what it's like to launch a brand in a category that is bulky and leaky and that many thought would never sell online. We wanted to know the story of the company, why eComm, and how they address the most obvious of hurdles—shipping products in these tough categories—because it all starts with the packaging.

Drew didn't launch his company with the idea of being just another laundry detergent on the shelf. In fact, the company was making a product that would clean and protect surfaces and equipment for athletes when they realized that if their product was safe and effective on these plastic, synthetic surfaces, why not formulate it for cleaning modern synthetic clothes?

"People think we're insane for going into laundry. They asked, 'How are you going to compete with Tide?' But we're not. We have an opportunity in a static category to provide a new chemistry that cleans differently. We're not relying on fragrance to mask odor but on new chemistry to really get at the source. We believe we can enter the space with a radically different product."

Part of HEX's radical difference came in the form of their packaging: a pouch with a spout rather than the traditional laundry detergent bottle. The pack differentiation excited retail store buyers and got HEX on store shelves, but consumers didn't necessarily take to the new packaging. Looking back, Drew acknowledges that maybe they didn't need to innovate on every aspect of their product, because what was inside was most important. "We believe that clean is the absence of things you don't want in your fabric, not just smelling like detergent fragrance." Most brands haven't changed over the years, but fabrics have, and truly getting the stink out (rather than masking it) is the foundation of HEX's success.

But back to the packaging. While the spouted pouches seemed like a great solution to bulky bottles that are hard to ship, Westervelt admits, "We didn't do consumer research to determine if the package was acceptable to the consumer. We later realized consumers may want new and different, but don't hate the bottle. On the shelf, people did not recognize the pouch as laundry detergent." So Drew began looking again at more traditional packaging, but in this case, optimized for eComm.

What exactly does that mean? It could be any combination of optimization measures: a pack of one or two bottles, not a case of six; a unit size less than 50 ounces, not 100 ounces; or some additional safeguards like thicker cardboard, additional cardboard stabilizers, a cap that fits perfectly and tightly, and maybe even a dab of glue under that cap.

While it sounds simple, it can be challenging to find production and packaging partners that have all the necessary components and the ability to go the extra mile with these safety measures. For this change, Drew looked at some successful brands and also called in the pros. He advises, "If you don't have the right product, you can try to be bullish and pioneering and do it yourself, or you can save a lot of time and money by talking to people who have experience."

So why go to these lengths when a brand can develop a perfectly respectable business on the retail shelf?

Like other brands tell us, Amazon is a powerful place to tell your story, get the right eyes on your brand through targeted marketing, and get candid customer feedback. Soon enough, Drew will know whether the packaging changes have been a hit or they need further tweaking to improve the user experience.

"As a new brand, you have to take [consumer feedback] for what it's worth, and use it when it shows you what you can improve. At the end of the day, it doesn't matter what I think; it matters what consumers think and what they want."

And if you are serious about making a product that is not about you but about your consumer, Drew's advice is: "Don't go buy 100,000 boxes until you learn. Buy 10,000 boxes. And expect the package to evolve." Amazon provides a great platform to test and learn, whether around product, pack, or marketing.

"It takes time to create content, takes time to perfect the product, and takes time to understand how to spend your money on Amazon to get consumer trial." We couldn't have said it better.

3

—⁆⁆⁆—

RELATIONSHIP
VS. AUTOMATION

I f you've advertised your brand extensively with Google, Facebook, or other self-managed platforms, you've probably experienced how big, scaled technology organizations are terrible at people and relationship management. They're just not designed for that sort of thing. Their algorithm-based information gathering, organization, and presentation are specifically structured to circumvent the need for human oversight as much as possible, for maximum scale and efficiency.

And Amazon is no exception. As with Google and Facebook, unless you're in the top tiers of sales or advertising spend, you'll have limited human interaction and support, if any. When human interaction *is* offered, it's generally a not-so-thinly veiled effort to help you spend more on the respective platform. After all, the service is ostensibly "free," and we all know there is no such thing.

Although thinking about human interaction isn't generally a priority for major tech organizations, it becomes a larger focus as they evolve. They are all increasing investments in human touch with various types of representatives, even though they're primarily there to help you advertise more. When you do have a contact, they're usually intelligent, well meaning, and knowledgeable about the platform's features, but in many cases, you'll be disappointed in their ability to meaningfully impact the areas of their company that might be causing you difficulty.

This is all to say that your success and profitability on these platforms is either your responsibility or the responsibility of the employees or agencies you've hired to handle the task.

On the positive side, this design for scale and automation also applies to the merchandising, marketing, and reporting tools you have access to, and all of them are improving at breakneck speed on Amazon. Once you become accustomed to the iterative release of new features and functionality, you'll appreciate the speed and flexibility these self-service options make available and the immediate impact they can have on your business.

Compare the effort it takes to list new products on Amazon to the effort it takes to get retail placements for those products in-store. Then compare how much each effort costs. On Amazon, you can have a new product live within hours, at negligible expense, with a campaign set up to drive relevant visitor traffic from all over the nation. It could take months or even years to achieve the same thing in brick-and-mortar, if you achieve it at all. And when it comes to costs, the online world presents many more opportunities than challenges—and the brands that get this are flourishing on Amazon.

So let's say you had access to a live person at Amazon. What would you ask them to do for you? Improve your product ranking? Remove a review you don't think is fair? Order more of your product? Give you some freebies? Listen to your fantastic idea for how Amazon could improve their business model? These might make *your* life easier, but remember, Amazon's reason for being is to serve the customer, and human interventions like these would undermine a valued customer's trust. On the other hand, when there's no human intervention on behalf of the vendor, there's a level playing field: the Amazon equi-system.

One of the best ways to familiarize yourself with this model is to become an expert at navigating Amazon's robust vendor and seller portals, where you can find everything you need to be successful on Amazon. And if one day you've grown your business to the point that you get a call or email from an Amazon employee, graciously accept any help and additional access they offer (and hold onto your wallet)!

4

---ᴑᴠᴑ---

VENDOR VS. SELLER

I n brick-and-mortar, there's typically one and only one way to sell to the retailer: the retailer chooses to stock your product and buys it from your company. At that point, they own it, and then pay you for it within the next 30 to 90 days. Margins, and resulting profitability for both you and the store, are pretty straightforward.

Amazon is different, not only due to factors like the aforementioned trade rates, but also because there are a few different ways to sell your product. As we dig into these, you'll quickly see the nuances and begin to understand that, though this business isn't turnkey, it provides even the smallest brands a path to success, if they just get it right for their business.

So what do we mean by "getting it right?"

When you get it right for Amazon, you're also getting it right for the broader eComm market, and this requires a well-thought-out strategy *before* you get to Amazon's door. One of the biggest, most common mistakes brands make when getting into eComm is thinking the platform is "brick-and-mortar online." To contrast all the differences, let's look at Amazon through the lens of traditional retail practices and outline the ways they've reinvented the experience.

We'll start with product, pricing, and profitability on both Vendor Central and Seller Central. These two business models have the same basic consumer-facing needs for content and promotion, but very different back-end dynamics for pricing and profitability. Here's a crash course on the differences.

AMAZON VENDOR CENTRAL

Most major CPG companies are well embedded in Amazon's vendor platform, the traditional selling model that they know best. The brand, also known as the vendor, sells product directly to Amazon, who then sells and ships the product to the consumer. In this model, the vendor pays a variety of fees—including co-op (trade), damage, freight, and quick pay terms—which are then deducted from vendor invoices each month. Within the vendor sales model, there are additional sub-platforms: Prime Pantry, Prime Now, Amazon Business, and Amazon Go. (And Amazon is always evolving, so there may be even more tomorrow!) As with retail stores, this is the simplest and most direct transaction: Amazon owns the product, which results in a largely hands-off management dynamic for the brand.

And this is where the parallels to traditional retail end.

First, you have to be invited to join Vendor Central, and invitations aren't easy to come by. Sometimes you're invited when you're a highly visible brand in the market but not currently doing business with Amazon. Or you can be invited if you're selling your product on the seller platform and Amazon witnesses your success. This is a common recruitment practice that requires brands to carefully consider whether they want to continue to do business as a seller or engage with Amazon as a vendor.

For a short time, Amazon offered Vendor Express, which enabled small brands to get in the game as vendors rather than sellers. In theory, the cost of entry was lower, and it was Amazon's mission to put extra attention toward these fledgling brands to facilitate their growth. In 2018, the Vendor Express model was abandoned, which might indicate that the amount of effort required wasn't worth the return on investment for Amazon.

In the Vendor Central selling model, it's crucial to understand that Amazon trade rates are typically higher than rates in traditional retail. With a combination of base accrual, damage allowance, freight allowance, quick pay discounts, and ongoing discounts for consumers in Amazon's popular Subscribe & Save program, total fees can exceed 30%. With the lean margins common for grocery products, it's easy to see how quickly a brand's profitability can be challenged without the right planning. This doesn't mean it's an impossible model for brands; it just means you need to plan for the inevitability of these costs.

In this model, Amazon sets the retail pricing, and that's where price matching with the market begins. As Amazon scours the internet with its automated web crawler, prices for your products may adjust daily or even hourly, depending on pricing in other retail locations.

Remember, Amazon isn't a low-price leader, but they're a fast follower.

Amazon won't abide by a minimum advertised price (MAP) policy when there are clearly lower prices in the market to be matched. It's their belief that the brand is responsible for control of their pricing strategy in the market, and if there's a lower price out there to match, they'll match it. It's ultimately the brand's responsibility to ensure price consistency and parity. This is why it's so important to have a well-executed MAP policy that starts at the source of your business, not when pricing equilibrium has already been upended in the market.

There are clear benefits to working with Amazon on their vendor platform. It's a traditional retail selling relationship that integrates well into a company's existing business model, and it has minimal challenges from an accounting or operations standpoint. It's a more hands-off management model for vendors, although few people with daily management responsibility for Amazon would say it is hands off, as Amazon offers challenges in other ways. But once we look at the Seller Central model, it's clear how much more engagement is required of the brand to make their Amazon business hum.

It used to be true that Vendor Central had a more robust variety of marketing programs. However, this has changed dramatically, as many of the best programs for smaller brands have migrated to the Seller Central platform. Coupons, Subscribe & Save, and Lightning Deals (to name a few)—which were once exclusively available on the vendor platform—are now also available to sellers. Some of the big-bucks promotions, like Amazon Family brand sponsorship, are currently available only on the vendor platform. But with price tags that can reach into seven figures, it's clear that these opportunities aren't for small brands anyway.

One benefit that's remained exclusively available to vendors is access to the sub platforms within Amazon. com—Prime Pantry, Prime Now, Amazon Go—and others are reserved for brands that sell directly to Amazon. This begs the question: with Amazon's mission to continue to grow, how will this change in the coming years? The current trend is towards functional parity between the selling models, but to what ultimate extent and on what timeline remains unclear. There are even whispers of a unified platform that may upend the current models!

So what are the downsides to Vendor Central?

First, the cost of pay to play is often out of range for small brands—it's even challenging to make this model work for large brands in the margin-starved food and beverage categories. When Jeff Bezos said, "*Your* margin is *my* opportunity," his critical eye was probably focused on the beefy margins in books, electronics, home and garden, and other categories. But this doesn't hold up as well in grocery, where margins are already set near the bone and there's so little to shave away.

Secondly, there is complete loss of brand pricing control. As brands implement traditional high/low promotions in retail, Amazon quickly tracks and matches those low prices, even if they're promotional prices, and even if you already give Amazon ongoing trade support. Not only can this erode your strategic price points on Amazon, it also infuriates brick-and-mortar retailers. And to add insult to injury, Amazon will likely ask you to make up the difference in their profitability from these painful price drops.

AMAZON SELLER CENTRAL

Amazon Seller Central is a third-party (3P) selling model on Amazon.com, managed by an independent seller. It could be the brand itself or a 3P seller that sets up a Storefront and purchases products to resell on Amazon. Products are listed on the Amazon site, but Amazon does not buy or own them. Within the Seller Central model, there are two sub models.

- **Fulfillment by Merchant (FBM)**

  With this Seller Central model, the brand lists their products on Amazon's website but ships the product directly to the consumer. The brand pays a small monthly seller fee and a referral fee, which varies by category but is typically around 15%. This is the only model on the seller platform that's available for perishable products. Sellers' products don't typically receive the Amazon Prime designation, but Amazon has launched a program called Seller-Fulfilled Prime where brands can qualify for Prime designation by meeting certain criteria in expedited order processing and shipping.

As the opportunities for perishable brands increase online, more and more fulfillment companies are specializing in shipping perishable products for Amazon sellers. They understand the Amazon rules of play and continually optimize their models to drive costs down. Their main areas of differentiation from other fulfillment agencies are the technology and packaging precision they use to determine the best options for a given product. Even the smallest tweaks to pack size and weight can have material impact on fulfillment costs and, ultimately, profitability for your brand.

- **Fulfillment by Amazon (FBA)**

  This Seller Central model is also managed by an independent 3P; the brand itself or a 3P seller. Product is owned by the seller, shipped into and stored in Amazon fulfillment centers, and shipped to the consumer by Amazon. Here as well, the brand pays a small monthly seller fee and a referral fee, which varies by category but is typically around 15%. Additionally, the brand pays Amazon fulfillment and storage fees, based on the size and weight of the product. Because of Amazon's scale and corresponding clout, it's widely believed that they do fulfillment better and cheaper than most other fulfillment alternatives. Product sold through FBA automatically receives the Prime designation, and because it's shipped by Amazon, the transaction is largely seamless for the consumer. Customers may not even realize they are purchasing from an FBA seller rather than buying directly from Amazon. The seller is paid by Amazon on a two-week cycle, with a complete statement of fees once the product sells to the consumer.

There are clear benefits to working with Amazon on their seller platform—the big one is control. First, as the seller, you control the amount of inventory shipped into Amazon's fulfillment centers, so there is no need to hope that Amazon orders the right amount of your special Halloween candy in time for trick-or-treaters. The inventory decision is up to you—be as conservative or aggressive as you want.

The other key area where the seller has control is pricing. Many brands have successfully maintained their premium image and price points by using the Seller Central model. This is impactful for the entire market, as a brand can strategically and successfully deploy pricing and promotions in all its sales channels without fear of Amazon slashing pricing and undermining their strategy.

Obviously, another *big* benefit is fulfillment. Amazon's sheer scale ensures that it receives the best rates and passes on at least a fraction of those benefits so that FBA fulfillment will make good financial sense for most sellers.

The seller platform also offers robust reporting, far more in-depth than on the vendor platform. Since the seller is the customer in this scenario, Amazon is mindful of providing tools for success that continue to draw brands and sellers to this platform.

As with most choices in life, there are some trade-offs. In this case, the big one is a higher level of day-to-day, hands-on management. You as the seller are responsible for using Amazon's self-serve portal for almost all elements of your business—from maintaining inventory to running promotions.

If you talk to 10 different Amazon experts, you may get 10 different opinions on the "best" way to go into business with Amazon: as a vendor, as a seller, or the hybrid model of using both platforms. Before Amazon began to enhance the Seller Platform, the common wisdom was that a brand could only realize their greatest potential by eventually becoming a vendor rather than a seller. But in 2017, sellers eclipsed vendors by selling 51% of total products on Amazon, for a whopping $130 billion in sales. (And remember, those are predictable, healthy profits for Amazon, since they pocket a guaranteed commission and fully covered fulfillment fees.) It's clear that Amazon is committed to bringing functional parity to the two platforms, which for practical purposes means bringing increased functionality to the seller side.

Given all of these benefits, why do most of the products of large CPG companies live on the vendor platform rather than Seller Central FBA? It boils down to a brand's ability to adapt to what is basically a consignment model, often a major digression from their existing business model and an insurmountable challenge for their finance team.

To optimize their business, some brands choose a hybrid approach. By operating on the seller platform, they can introduce new products and load in plenty of inventory for a successful launch. This is necessary because on the vendor side, the automated inventory management system tends to order small amounts and run out of stock until its algorithm begins to recognize demand for a new product. This can take weeks and sometimes months, all while a brand is expecting to make a huge splash with a new product. By launching simultaneously on the seller and vendor sides, you can help to build the demand by sales through the seller platform, which ultimately triggers the vendor in-stock system to ramp up orders. As recently as Q4 2018, we heard rumblings that Amazon may be restricting the ability to use the two models simultaneously in this hybrid approach. While the story is still developing at the time of publication of this book, this could be a tectonic shift in the way brands are able to do business and yet another example of the fundamental ways in which Amazon continues to change. Or not. You just never know with Amazon.

Also, let's say Amazon discontinues an item on the vendor platform because it's just not profitable for them, due to price matching with the market and resulting margin erosion. You can then list that product on Seller Central, set a fair but not rock-bottom price, and continue availability to the consumer. This, we believe, plays well with Amazon's philosophy of dedication to positive customer experience.

Amazon consumers shop for a variety of reasons—not just fair pricing, but also convenience, selection, and consistent availability. A product doesn't necessarily need to have rock-bottom pricing to have a successful life on Amazon, but shoppers don't like when the product they buy regularly simply disappears. They don't know that it has to do with the brand's profitability struggles with Amazon; they just know they can no longer get a product that they love. This is where the back-up function, which Seller Central plays so well, kicks in for the consumer and your brand.

In our business, we're witnessing brands launch exclusively on Amazon Seller Central more often than Vendor Central. With the expansion of benefits to the seller platform and the ability to maintain control over pricing and inventory, brands are now forging their own path forward, independent of the constraints of traditional selling models. Those that can't take on this level of account management are increasingly looking at an evolving business model that offers some of the same benefits with less hands-on management, such as working with a dedicated third-party seller.

How does this model work? The brand sells product directly to the third-party seller as if they were any distributor or retailer. In turn, that seller manages an Amazon 3P marketplace for multiple brands who contract with them. They're typically full-service, offering marketing management, uploading content supplied by the brand, and even assembling product bundles and variety packs. It's crucial to do your research of course, as functionality and costs vary widely, and that includes validating their seller rating on Amazon, which is a fairly reliable reflection of their reputation.

Another option to lighten the burden of the daily management of your Amazon business is to work with an Amazon-specific broker. There's a handful of good ones out there that have long-time expertise working with Amazon. If you pursue this option, do plenty of homework. Make sure the broker offers a solid, dedicated skill set in multiple areas—sales, marketing, and operations, for example—and that Amazon account management is their primary focus and not just a tack-on to a conventional brick-and-mortar brokerage hoping to get in on the Amazon explosion.

PREPARE

5

—◦◦◦—

IS YOUR PRODUCT RIGHT FOR ECOMM?

When brands launch online, they often just slap their existing product assortment on Amazon and wait for it to fly off the virtual shelf. It doesn't take long for disappointment to set in with the realization that there's more to this online game than they thought. Then comes the question about whether Amazon is the right path for them.

What if we reverse this order and start with that last question: Is your product right for Amazon?

It is? Great! Now, just a few more questions…

- Is it the right size and the right pack count *for the consumer?*
- Will it be shipped in its case? If so, will the outer case withstand the UPS/USPS/FedEx shipping process?

- Will it work well as a subscription item (a highly consumed product with a 30–90-day usage cadence)?
- Will it possibly break, spill, or leak in transit?
- Will prohibitive weight be an obstacle to shipping costs?
- If your product needs to be prepped or broken down to the unit level, are you prepared to pay Amazon's preparation fees for this additional handling?

And these are just some of the things you need to know about product in the planning process for eComm. But don't be dismayed—there are solutions!

The ideal products for Amazon are designed as Ships in Own Container (SIOC) and qualify for Amazon's Frustration-Free Packaging (FFP) certification. By having SIOC products, you'll be well on your way to FFP product standards as well as setting yourself up for participation in Amazon's popular subscription program, if applicable.

How do these dovetail? Here is Amazon's definition (Amazon.com) of FFP: "Certified Frustration-Free Packaging is recyclable and comes without excess packaging materials. The product inside is the same, and everything is included in the Certified Frustration-Free Packaging that would be in the original manufacturer's packaging."

SIOC takes this one step further by ensuring that products are, by design, the right product with the right pack count in a package that can be shipped as is because it is designed to withstand the rigors of shipping.

FFP was launched in 2008 in response to products shipped in packaging necessary for retail shelf sales but not online sales. A perfect example of this is the plastic clamshell, an essential deterrent to theft in brick-and-mortar, but a waste of packaging in eComm. On the other end of the spectrum were companies that overwrapped, to ensure that their easily spilled or fragile products arrived intact. Customers also saw this as wasteful and pushed back.

But over time, FFP has evolved into a broad term that applies to more than recyclability and over-packaging. There has to be the right balance of protective packaging, product integrity, and positive consumer experience by neither over-packaging nor scrimping on protection that can literally make or break the integrity of your product once it's delivered. We always advise clients to meet the standards of FFP, even if they're not seeking the certification. It's simply best practice.

But when you're creating a pack to the FFP and SIOC standard, don't get too fancy devising a way to use the outer packaging as a billboard for your product. Most products, with the exception of extreme oversized cases (like paper towels), will be shipped in an Amazon box, ensuring that their iconic smile logo appears on front porches near and far.

When determining the right size and right pack, consider positive consumer experience first. You might think an individual unit is the best option, and that seems logical until you consider the math. With the cost of shipping *anything* in the $4–$5 range, you can understand why the economics of shipping, say, a single can of frosting is not profitable for Amazon in the vendor model or for you in the seller model. Consumers willingly shop for multi-unit packs on Amazon. This makes even more sense for the consumer using the highly successful Subscribe & Save program Amazon created years ago, which continues to be one of its top initiatives for consumables. Think of this as the ultimate loyalty program: Prime shoppers are loyal, but Prime shoppers who are subscription shoppers are the gold standard in customer loyalty.

Subscribers get discounts when they sign up for regularly delivered product, and suddenly well-loved and highly consumed items become attractive to buy in multiples. If your product works as part of Subscribe & Save, this should be a key consideration when designing them and their packaging. Product usage should fall within a 30–90-day cadence, so the combination of unit measure and pack count is integral to the conversation.

Like the Club Store Channel, special packs in eComm are a fundamental way to differentiate your product and ensure you're meeting the needs of the Amazon shopper. It's commonly believed that special eComm packs will also shield you from Amazon's sophisticated price-mapping tool in the vendor model (which price matches "like" products on competitive retailer sites in real time). However, Amazon now conducts price matching at the unit count, and even the unit measure level, so that protection is no longer assured.

As Amazon's business has evolved, simply providing a different pack count is not enough to differentiate for price-matching protection, so more and more brands are turning to entirely unique products or new flavor and scent variations. This doesn't mean special packs and multiple-unit packs are not essential to your Amazon plan or that it's not important to provide a pack size that meets unique online-consumer buying habits. It just means that it won't necessarily protect you against price comparison and associated declines if your pricing in the rest of the market activates price drops on Amazon.

So how do you manage this pricing–matching issue to protect your brand and business with other retail partners? We cover some of the best ways to do this in the next chapter.

6

PRICING & PROFITABILITY

P ricing is probably the trickiest component of your Amazon business to manage. This is true whether you're selling on the vendor platform, where Amazon's automated system sets your price through its highly sophisticated algorithms, or whether you set the price as the seller of record on the Amazon seller platform.

There's also a third component that you may have little control over, and that's the impact of third-party sellers purchasing your product and reselling it on Amazon. Trying to manage this can be a nonstop, frustrating game of whack-a-mole. But no matter what dynamic is affecting your business, understanding and doing your best to mitigate it without entirely losing your sanity is key. So first, let's look at pricing in both Vendor Central and Seller Central.

PRICING

As you know, in this model, you're selling product to Amazon as the retail customer. Amazon buys the product from you, sets the price, sells the product, and ships it to the consumer. As you also know, pricing is at their sole discretion, so you're treading into dangerous legal territory if you try to engage in pricing conversations with Amazon (assuming you even have access to an Amazon Vendor Manager). Never before has there been greater opportunity for consumers, and greater challenges for brands, as in this new arena of complete and ubiquitous visibility into pricing.

And if you're a brand selling on the vendor platform, you get constant feedback from your retail partners in other channels, and it's usually not positive. But, as we've noted, attractive pricing is only one of the drivers of online purchases; Amazon consumers are in it for more than just the lowest price, yet it's the strategy component that can have the biggest impact on your brand, its profitability, and equity in the balance of the market. This dynamic spurs successful online brands to treat eComm much as they do the Club Channel, where special packs produce strong sales results and minimize impact on their other retail channels. So let's explore how pricing, in conjunction with the right product and product packs, can work to take your online success to a new level.

We'll look at this in the context of both Vendor Central and Seller Central—different models with different implications for pricing and profitability.

At Amazon, it's not unusual for a single product to have several price changes within a year, a week, or even a day! On the Vendor Central platform, there are more than 2.5 million real-time price changes daily. And again, Amazon is not the low-price leader, but its technology makes it a fast follower of its market competitors. With Amazon's price-mapping technology, combined with a team of human eyes on the job dedicated to visual product comparison—and now, a team that also makes store visits—it's hard to escape the impact of this pricing machine. Add the new dynamic of Amazon's complete visibility into your product pricing at Whole Foods, and it's easy to see why pricing is such a pain point for many brands. Amazon's philosophy is simple: you, the manufacturer, control your pricing in the market, and if there's a lower price out there, you've created the need for Amazon to match it.

This is why Amazon won't agree to a minimum advertised price (MAP) policy. It doesn't matter if the price being matched is a short-term promotional price or that the co-op funding you provide Amazon levels the playing field. If your product is available at a discount to consumers through a different retailer and that price appears on Amazon's radar, that discounted price becomes Amazon's everyday price for the duration of the promotion. This strategy is at the heart of Amazon's consumer-centric philosophy, which has defined its leadership.

Let's say Amazon sells a four-pack of potato chips for $20, with subscribers receiving an additional 5%–15%

discount. Target has the same potato chips on sale for the month of March at the equivalent price of $3 per unit. Amazon will now match $3 as the everyday price and lower your pack price to $12, while continuing to extend the 5%–15% discount to subscribers. That variance of $8 has now dramatically degraded the potato chip brand's profitability with Amazon, which puts the brand in jeopardy of being discontinued.

In this scenario, Amazon will make a funding request of the brand, or the ASIN [Amazon Standard Identification Number] will be discontinued (a process affectionately known as CRAP out, for "can't realize a profit"). Amazon has automated this funding request through their vendor portal, asking brands to make them whole by a specified amount in order to continue to be profitable and maintain placement on Amazon.com.

And remember, although witnessing pricing volatility is challenging and it's tempting to try and do something about it, it's important to steer clear of pricing conversations, lest you wander into legally dubious territory. So go into the selling relationship with eyes wide open about pricing and its impact on profitability—for both you and Amazon—its impact on other valued retail partners, and your limited ability to develop and enforce a MAP policy with Amazon.

That doesn't mean you should rule out a MAP policy. It just means you'll need to manage your MAP across all channels and start at the source: your distributors and other retail accounts that you sell to directly. This is often a painful process that requires stressful conversations with long-time valued partners. You may not get everything you want in these negotiations, but that doesn't mean you should give up and let your pricing strategy be completely upended.

There are technologies and firms that can track violators and help you to enforce your policy. It's ultimately up to the brand how strictly they want to manage their policy, which could mean in extreme cases declining to sell to an egregious violator. We've seen a client decline a $30,000 purchase order to a retailer that had previously wrought pricing havoc in the market by selling on Amazon. That was a gutsy move, but it had positive long-term results with both their Amazon relationship and the broader market.

Ultimately, vendors are expected to take responsibility for Amazon's profitability of their brand within the Amazon ecosystem. There are many creative ways to support profitability—strategies for merchandising, marketing, unique online packs, careful curation of product gross margins, and efficiencies around cost to serve, to name a few. Pricing strategy has suddenly become much more complex, so putting in the work up front to develop a true strategy and manage this element of your business has a big, long-term upside. And it's far easier to manage early on than it is to try and walk back miles of mistakes.

Pricing is where the two models—Vendor Central and Seller Central—begin to really diverge from one another. In the Seller Central model, you set your retail price and Amazon can't change it. Period. That said, it is worth noting that in late 2018, Amazon began exerting pressure on brands in the Seller Central platform to match lower prices found on other websites, particularly Walmart and Jet, as competition heats up between the 800-pound eCommerce gorilla and the brick-and-mortar juggernaut ironically playing the upstart role in the online world. This pressure is coming in the form of a Buy Box suppression in the event that Amazon finds a lower price elsewhere—even if there are no other Amazon sellers on your listing. (The Buy Box is the seller's listing that "wins" as the default to add to cart or purchase on a given listing page.)

Though your item will still be for sale on Amazon, the listing becomes confusingly presented, so that many customers may not realize the item is still for sale. (Since there is no active Buy Box listing, and the customer has to click further into the available sellers section to figure out how to purchase.) So even though Amazon is not actually reducing your prices as on the vendor side, or specifically requiring you to lower your price, they are impacting your sales velocity as pressure to lower pricing, or improve management of pricing outside of Amazon, as previously discussed.

Obviously, you'll be setting your pricing based on vital criteria around the right price point for your product, as well as factoring in the cost of fulfillment, whether by you or by Amazon in the popular FBA model. Also, whether handling fulfillment yourself or using FBA, be sure to consider the impact of Amazon's referral fee. Even with these additional costs, the seller platform is often more profitable for brands, because you're now working with all of the dollars in between cost of goods and retail price, rather than cost of goods and wholesale price to Amazon in the vendor model—essentially, more dollars to play with to cover these seller-associated costs.

The most challenging products, whether on the vendor or seller platform, are those that are heavy or oversized and have a low retail price point. We've seen fulfillment fees as high as $30 on a five-gallon product, but in that case, the relative value, generous product profit margin, and ultimate price point were high enough that the product was still highly profitable. This is not usually the case. You have to understand the numbers as you work to set the best price for your product, both for you and for the consumer. Remember: it doesn't need to be a rock-bottom price, just a fair one.

PROFITABILITY

Once upon a time, Amazon wanted to be "The Everything Store" and was most interested in serving the top line of its business. This strategy worked well, and Amazon revenue grew (Statista, 2017) from less than $7 billion in 2004 to $177 billion in 2017. But since right around 2014, when its top-line attention expanded to include bottom-line focus, profitability has become Amazon's drumbeat, forever changing the Vendor Central dynamic for brands.

We've mentioned that profitability is the responsibility of brands themselves; even after negotiating an annual trade plan, you may be asked by Amazon throughout the year for additional funding to cover unprofitable products.

Although there could be several factors contributing to the unprofitability of a particular item, and price matching is one of them, shipping is another major driver. According to Statista, in 2016, even with $99 annual Prime fees collected from over 65 million Prime members (Statista, Number of Amazon Prime Members in US), Amazon's shipping revenue was $8.98 billion and outbound shipping costs were $16.17 billion, a gap of over $7 billion (Statista, Amazon's Shipping Revenue and Outbound Shipping Costs, 2006-2016, 2017). In May of 2018, Amazon raised its Prime membership fee to $119 in an attempt to close that gap. If you're planning to sell an item that's low cost and high weight, you will want to consider whether that profitability profile makes it right for eComm.

It's absolutely essential to understand Amazon's profitability measures as they relate to your brand *before* you make decisions about moving forward with your Amazon relationship *and* your choice of selling platforms—vendor, seller, or both. In eComm, percent margin is irrelevant. Amazon is most concerned about the actual dollars a product or brand contributes to the bottom line. You'll hear a lot about CP (contribution profit) and CPPU (contribution profit per unit), and that makes sense when you consider that the key variable of shipping, which is different for every product, impacts profitability in eComm but not in a traditional retail store.

And the inevitable question "What margin does Amazon require?" is best answered with a bowling ball/basketball example.

Take a 17-pound bowling ball and a 1.5-pound basketball. They're the same size and occupy the same space on a retail shelf. So in a store, the required retail profit margin percentage for both should be similar. But with the dramatic difference in their weights, and with shipping being the big factor in eComm profitability, can Amazon realistically require the same "percentage" margin delivered by the vendor for these two very different products? Shipping cost has to be factored into the contribution profit equation, and needless to say, more dollars need to be available in the bowling ball margin than the basketball margin.

The additional costs of doing business with Amazon on the vendor platform—trade co-op, freight allowance, damage allowance, merchandising program spending, coupon fees, Amazon Media Group spending, and other forms of support—may also be viewed in a positive way by Amazon as contributors to your overall brand profitability.

The goal here is not only to provide some clarity around pricing and profitability, but also to reveal the complexity of this topic. Above all, do your research! And before you enter unknown territory, with variables you can't anticipate or questions you can't answer, hire a professional who's fully immersed in this business to help you navigate, so you don't get lost there.

FIXING A BROKEN BUSINESS

In 2015, Marti was tasked with getting a small and languishing Amazon business on track for her company, a major player with multiple brands in a variety of snack categories. New to the eComm channel herself, she quickly ramped up her knowledge by reaching out to experts in the field, but the turn-around and huge success she achieved—taking a half-million-dollar business to an eleven-million-dollar business in three years—was largely her own.

How did she accomplish this? She dug into the fundamentals of the business. "I would sit on the couch at night with my husband and we would go through each ASIN and fix it." This meant hundreds of ASINs—scraping content, realigning products in the right categories, and adjusting replenishment settings. We can only envision how tedious but necessary this process was.

Next, pricing was a mess. Amazon was given incorrect pricing from the start that was cut to the bone. Without funding available for marketing, the business was never going to grow. Working with her Amazon Vendor Manager, assigned to a big brand with a small business, they were able to work out a pricing structure that made sense for both Amazon and the company, enabling the investment in the brand that Amazon values.

At this point, the company had to lean in with marketing and investment in the brands. "We did a promotion for New Year/New You with new eComm four-packs. The [return on investment] was horrible, but it had to be done and now these packs are the top sellers."

In addition to their role in eComm packaging, the operations team was a key player in this success story. First, they consolidated all brands that had been shipping from multiple manufacturing plants into one shipping location (mixing center) for Amazon orders. Next, they worked on shortening shipment lead time from seven days to Amazon's required three days. Consolidating products dramatically increased the size of the purchase orders (POs) and decreased the number of POs and their destinations, as well as minimizing the sheer chaos that can result from shipping multiple product lines from numerous warehouses into hundreds of Amazon fulfillment centers.

In order to develop a plan to meet Amazon's three-day lead time, Marti got all stakeholders into one room for a day and walked out with a plan to move to the necessary timeframe, beginning the following Monday. Working closely with the operations team was instrumental in not just having a well-oiled supply chain but also a profitable business.

"Amazon's supply chain was never trying to make money off of us. Using their cross-dock program and agreeing to their pick-up allowance proved not only to be efficient but also cost effective. In 2017, our channel profitability was higher than the company average." Marti's experience underscores the importance of understanding the financial model of your Amazon business and its departure from brick-and-mortar assumptions.

When you're managing multiple brands on Amazon, it's not unusual to have a huge catalog, so it wasn't surprising when Marti was challenged by her company to validate selling 500+ items. Knowing how long-tail items have a welcome home and some of the greatest success online, she had her finance team analyze each item. Out of the entire mix, only 20 were unprofitable and needed to be jettisoned. This can be credited to getting the basics right, conducting a thorough catalog scrub, and the ongoing maintenance of clean and accurate listings.

Marti's experience is a perfect case study of how walking into Amazon without a plan can result in a stagnating, unprofitable business that cannot afford to grow without a major overhaul. This is the point at which many brands get frustrated with Amazon, pick up their ball, and go home.

Thankfully for this company, Marti understood the value of digging into the basics, developing a plan, getting involved in all aspects of the business to have the right products in the right packs at the right price, and optimizing cost to serve. And most important, persevering.

7

PLACEMENT: YOUR CONTENT IS YOUR SHELF

Sometimes, when people talk about placement online, they're referring to the category or the Amazon selling platform you choose. For us, placement means the shelf—in this case, the virtual shelf. When optimizing your presence in a brick-and-mortar store, it's all about the shelf. Does the product look good? Is it abundant and well merchandised? Are display materials in good shape? Where does it appear? Is it at eye level? Are there several facings?

But online, your shelf presence is your onsite content. It can be brilliant and ever-present, and since it is virtual, it can never be trashed by competitors who may rip down your shelf-talker in the store. This content enables you to engage with the consumer like never before. Online, your product page is your most powerful tool, and Amazon provides plenty of opportunities to maximize impact through a variety of carefully crafted components.

You can convey your brand story through multiple images, videos, and hundreds of words more than a single in-store merchandising piece allows. And all of this opportunity calls for best practices in these key areas:

- Product title
- Images and videos
- Basic product detail (five bullet points and a description)
- Enhanced brand content

PRODUCT TITLE

The product title is the most important message to your consumer for two reasons: it's the first thing they read to understand your product, and it indexes highest in Amazon's search. This is why accuracy and relevancy matter so much. Here you have to balance your desire for the absolute best search results by stuffing your title with every viable term you can think of, and creating a superior consumer experience that enables them to easily read and understand what they're buying. And these two goals are often in conflict.

Think about it: Have you ever tried to purchase something on Amazon and haven't been able to tell whether you were buying one unit or twelve? Have you ever had to read through a 50-word product title more than once to try to understand what you were getting? It's not uncommon, because titles are often so poorly written and so packed with search terms, they're barely comprehensible to the shopper. Just as searches can bring shoppers to your absolutely perfect product, confusing product titles and descriptions can quickly drive them away.

Product descriptors (search terms) that are important to the consumer should be used to full advantage. For some brands, this means words like "organic," "plant-based," "gluten free," and "peanut-free" are key differentiators that shoppers look for specifically. At the same time, phrases like "the best ever" or "you'll love the taste" in a product title are generic turn-offs. Most importantly, don't forget to declare the brand name, product and pack size in your product title. Next time you're on Amazon, read the one-star reviews and see for yourself how many are written by buyers who didn't get the pack size they expected. Usually, these reviews have nothing to do with the product quality, because when a consumer feels cheated or tricked, quality takes a back seat. And that one-star review, by the way, stays put and impacts your overall rating.

IMAGES AND VIDEOS

Images and videos are a hugely impactful way to convey what your consumer is receiving. If you're selling a 12-pack of candy bars, your primary image should show a 12-pack instead of a single candy bar. Amazon provides additional slots to the left of the main product image for secondary images, where you have a chance to communicate more about your brand. The common move for many brands is to use these image slots to show the product pack from seven different angles, which is a sad waste of an opportunity. Yes, it's helpful to have one shot of your ingredient label, but here you can be more creative and informative. You can showcase your brand in lifestyle shots, create helpful infographics when some instruction is needed, or even show your relevant and impressive brand certifications. And here's where you can add a short video that tells your story.

BASIC PRODUCT DETAIL: 5 BULLETS & PRODUCT DESCRIPTION

Basic content is the information you can easily see on a product page, living above the fold. Right under the primary and secondary photos is an area where you can list up to five bullet points. This is where the top selling features and benefits of your product should be listed. It may very well be the last information the consumer reads about your product, since a lot of shoppers won't scroll lower than that to make a buying decision.

Bullets should be concise and informative and put your best brand foot forward. This is another area where content creators can go overboard with packing in search terms, creating an avalanche of information that the consumer will never read. Again, this is where smart brand marketers balance the desire to cram in every possible keyword with the customer experience. Bullet points that aren't inviting and can't be read at a glance just don't get read. If a consumer has to use the drop-down arrow to read all five points, they're too long. Keep it simple, relevant, and interesting.

Right below the bullet points is an area for a more expanded description, where motivated consumers go to find more detail.

ENHANCED BRAND CONTENT

Even though only a small percentage of Amazon consumers scroll below the fold to look at enhanced brand content (also known as A+ content on the Vendor Central platform), this is a must-have for brands that are taking their Amazon opportunity seriously. Not only is this a place to truly showcase your brand's story, it's also another opportunity to develop content loaded with search terms. Don't underestimate the power of this additional beauty content on conversion.

SPEAKING THE LANGUAGE

K9 Natural pet food is one of our favorite Amazon success stories, and it all starts thousands of miles away from us in New Zealand. We talked to Jo O'Sullivan and Maddy Surie about what it's like to be an international brand selling on Amazon in the US, how they made the decision to jump into the eComm arena, and whether they would share with us their path to success.

K9 Natural has been selling in US stores since 2008. The company saw that there was a real demand for premium meat-based products in our pet-centric culture, so their first stop was with premium pet stores. In 2013, they launched on Amazon Vendor Central and over time started to focus on this channel for all the best reasons. As Jo put it, "It is really powerful for us being an exporter. Amazon gives us a platform to expose our brand to new customers. Since we are a natural, premium product, it is important for us to tell our story of the benefits of feeding a high-meat diet to your pets." However, by relying on retailers to tell their brand story, they realized a lot could be lost in translation, and the ability to connect with those retailers that need to tell it was geographically challenging.

They realized that consumers are changing rapidly and don't necessarily have time to go into a pet store or to haul large bags of dog food that could instead be delivered to their front door. Not surprisingly, pet products is one of the biggest categories online, and continues to be one of the fastest growing.

By 2016, Jo and Maddy began a more intent focus on their Amazon business, which resulted in making a pivotal and potentially scary decision for their brand. They left the Vendor Central selling platform and moved their business to Seller Central FBA. Vendor Central just wasn't the right place for their premium brand. Even though it enabled them to tell their story and connect with new consumers, they realized the lack of control over pricing devalued their brand and threatened to initiate a race to the bottom.

In January 2017, they crossed over from being an Amazon vendor to an Amazon seller. "We had to be brave about moving the business from Vendor Central to Seller Central, since we already had a substantial business on Amazon and didn't know what it would be like to be a seller." But having done their research, they knew this would enable them to take a step back and evaluate exactly how to reach people without having others control their destiny. They began by optimizing their content to not just tell their story but also to get traction with new customers. They were mindful to frame content for the US consumer and worked with consultants and others who challenged them to "think like Americans." Maddy noticed a change very quickly. "When we optimized our listings, we saw quite a jump in sales. It was quite incredible."

We asked if being an international company presented any challenges with Brand Registry. Whether because of their international status or not, it was quite a complex process, but it was ultimately worthwhile, because previously other sellers were able to take over their listings with less than optimal content, and now they are in control. There are still other 3Ps (and won't there always be?), but K9 is now the dominant seller of their own products, and with Brand Registry their content gets priority for their listings as well as the listings of third parties.

So how is it going? Each month is a record sales month for K9. In fact, business is so good that they're sometimes caught by surprise and run out of stock at Amazon's fulfillment centers. This is a challenge, since it can take Amazon up to a couple of weeks to process a shipment and make the product available for sale. But K9 is now able to reach a much broader geographic base than they did in their retail channels. They've built in-house capabilities to manage their Amazon business, because without a doubt, Seller Central has proven to be more hands-on than Vendor Central.

While this might seem like quite an investment for the brand, Jo says that "by allocating a resource we are actually cutting a lot of cost out of the business. By the time we ship to the US, ship to a distributor who ships to a store, there are lots of people taking cuts of our profitability. In this model, we ship to our US warehouse and directly into Amazon. One person managing this business from NZ versus multiple people on the ground in America is a much more profitable model for us."

When we asked Jo and Maddy their advice for other international brands, they told us, "Don't be afraid of the distance. It doesn't matter that we are in New Zealand. Even though we are miles away, we can manage it as if we were right in the US, which is a big advantage. We could not manage our traditional stores and distributors the same way."

Being open-minded was another huge asset. "We needed to think about how we could change and grow our brand rather than thinking we know everything because we know our brand and our products. We recognize that this channel is different. We have been quite clear and quite ambitious about what we want Amazon to deliver, so you need to be clear about your expectations and plan for the long term."

The last piece of their tale we want to tell is about the impact on their other retail channels. "Brick-and-mortar stores were scared of Amazon, but we proved we have actually enhanced their business. People might sometimes buy on Amazon and sometimes want a store connection or a local connection, and they are already educated about our product from Amazon. So there is a place for both."

8

---◉◉◉---

HOW TO WIN ON AMAZON

Your initial strategy in the first year, (and beyond, depending on your level of success) can be described as "moving the Amazon flywheel." At first, your business will be like an overpacked car with an empty gas tank, sitting immobile in your driveway. Your goal is to fuel that car up, check the oil, get the tire pressure right for the load it's bearing, and get it rolling down the road. That takes a lot of initial effort, but once you've got momentum on your side, it gets easier.

Amazon Ranking Factors

Though optimizing your product listings as discussed in the previous section is foundational, required, and the element most within your control, in and of itself, it's not enough to ensure long-term success for your business.

Amazon's A9 ranking algorithm is the key to your business's success. The exact makeup of this algorithm is, of course, not public knowledge, but its general features are fairly well understood. Some are important as direct ranking factors, and others are more helpful in actually converting the customer to buy, which then feeds into the other ranking factors.

In the 1990s, search engines crawled and indexed the world wide web based on the information they found on those pages—trusting the websites were legitimate—and made them visible to searchers accordingly. As you can imagine, spam (results that were irrelevant or incorrect based on the search) became rampant, with crafty webmasters "stuffing" unrelated keywords to garner as much traffic as they could. This was a bad experience for searchers, who ended up on sites irrelevant to their searches (often pornographic, as you can imagine!).

Then Google changed the game. Instead of blindly trusting the website's own publisher, they began requiring validation from *other, external* websites to corroborate what the website owner claimed their content to be about. That's when optimizing your own website became "necessary but not sufficient" to rank on Google.

On Amazon, the ranking factors are different, but the core concept is the same. You *must* first utilize all the merchandising opportunities that Amazon provides in the product-listing dashboard to present any and all relevant information as comprehensively as possible. However, in most cases, that's not enough by itself to rank for relevant searches.

To be clear and unambiguous from the start, *sales velocity is the single most important factor for your ranking on Amazon.*

The second core component for both ranking and converting to sale is customer feedback—specifically, the quantity and average star rating of your customer reviews.

These two factors predominantly determine your prominence in product ranking and therefore success on Amazon. And they should be looked at in *relative terms compared to your competition.* For example, 20 reviews may not be much in some categories, but they may be enough to best the competitors in your product category (for now!).

SALES VELOCITY

Sales velocity is defined by Amazon as "the number and dollar amount of a seller's transactions during any given month (Amazon Seller Central, 2018)" and is the single most important factor for your ranking success on Amazon. Also importantly, it cannot really be "gamed" in any reliable way, and especially not over the long term. Sales velocity must be earned, with sound marketing and brand-building efforts, both on and off Amazon. What does sales velocity mean, and how does it come into play?

Imagine searching on Amazon for "red Nike shoes." Amazon identifies 217 relevant product listings. In what order does it decide to present those listings as a result of your search?

If you guessed by "relative sales velocity," you're right. The sales velocity of your product determines the prominence of your listing compared to the other relevant listings in a given search. That's a bit of an oversimplification, but focusing on this will serve you well.

So is it that because your sales are highest, you'll appear first? Or because you appear first, your sales are highest? It's a chicken-and-egg situation: how can you increase sales when doing so requires increasing sales? The answer is marketing, which can come in a variety of forms both off and on Amazon. (And there are plenty of opportunities within Amazon's own platform to drive your traffic acquisition efforts. More about those later.)

The bottom line: it's up to you to get your car fueled up before it can take you anywhere. But that initial effort can reap great rewards as you earn your stars (literally and figuratively!) on Amazon.

PRODUCT REVIEWS

Third-party testimony at its most powerful, product reviews are an essential component of your success, both on and offline. No matter where consumers buy your product these days, their research usually begins online. In fact, various publicly available data show that roughly half of consumer product searches begin on Amazon, eclipsing Google and any other originating source. Google is the #1 search engine for questions like "How do I bathe my cat?" while Amazon has become its counterpart, where we look for products with intent to buy. This is primarily because of the product reviews we love to peruse, and all the ways previously discussed that Amazon makes purchasing fast and easy.

Amazon is widely known and respected among consumers as one of the most comprehensive, helpful, and even entertaining resources of unbiased customer feedback (do a Google search for "funny Amazon reviews" when you're bored). This is why many customers seek out Amazon reviews about a product they're thinking of buying, even when they're planning to buy it elsewhere (but often end up buying on Amazon anyway).

Amazon earned this reputation early in its existence, and it's long been one of the core differentiating features that keep customers returning again and again.

So as you can imagine, the quantity and quality of reviews for *your* products on Amazon are critical components of your success or failure on the platform – *and even for your brand as a whole*, since again, consumers will often check Amazon reviews when purchasing elsewhere. For those of you who've somehow not discovered this fact, there is no hiding from consumers on the internet, and especially on Amazon. You might be able to control the content on your website, but Amazon is an open forum where you don't have this control, which is why customers trust the feedback they find there and specifically seek that collective opinion about your product.

According to Channel Advisor's Consumer Shopping Habits Survey, when consumers shop online, 92% begin by reading product reviews and 84% trust reviews as much as recommendations from friends (LocalBright Consumer Review Survey, 2017). Shoppers seek out reviews; they want to know what people who've bought and tried your product think, and whether or not they'll buy it again. Never before has a single consumer-driven action had this kind of immediate weight and capability to catapult a new brand to success. In the days before eComm and social media, consumers who bought your product in a store could love it or hate it but you might never know exactly what they thought or why. Now, one product review can reach the entire world, and the impact this has on your brand reputation cannot be overstated.

Products with reviews between 4 and 5 stars need 40% less traffic to convert to a sale. On the other end of this phenomenon, one negative review can snowball quickly into an avalanche of criticism, creating a difficult trend to reverse. And many consumers believe that a product with a rating below 4 stars is a complete dud. That's why it's increasingly important to monitor and manage your Amazon reviews. As the brand, it's your job to respond to consumers, encourage them to reach out to you, and whenever possible, turn a negative review into an unexpected positive story. You won't get a lot of help from Amazon if you want a review removed that you believe is unfair. Unless it is fraudulent or completely unrelated to your brand, Amazon will not betray consumer trust by removing a cranky yet legitimate review.

Product reviews obviously impact your product ranking and, as shoppers, we all know how important it is to appear at the top. A whopping 70% (CPC Strategy 2018 Amazon Shopper Behavior Study) of buyers do not go past the first page, which means essentially the top 5 items on a particular landing page from a product search.

Right about now, you might be wondering how to get reviews to help your product sell when your product isn't selling because you need more reviews! Like sales velocity, it's another chicken-and-egg conundrum, and it's a hurdle you have to anticipate and overcome with initial investment.

First, let's cover how *not* to accumulate customer reviews. Never, ever review a product if you're an employee of that company, even on your personal Amazon account from your home computer. The consequences vary, but there are definitely consequences. One of our clients had their product reviewed by a legitimate frequent user. Amazon politely notified him that they would not be posting his review because of his ties to the company, where he had been employed three years prior!

In another case, a client didn't heed our warning and had employees post some perky reviews, which remained on-site until Amazon simply shut down their seller account. They are now out of business on Amazon. If this seems harsh, look at it from Amazon's perspective: the most important relationship customers have with Amazon is their fundamental trust in the company. If reviews are viewed as inauthentic, that fundamental trust is broken. And if you think Amazon won't figure it out, you're underestimating the sophistication of their technology.

Gaining reviews has become more difficult since Amazon began allowing customers to opt out of seller communication. A lot of customers are taking advantage of this option, which automatically rejects any attempt to communicate about an order. Many customers allow the requests, however, so it's still your best opportunity to generate reviews.

Amazon does offer some options to obtain legitimate reviews. On the vendor platform, the Amazon Vine program enables you to provide samples for up to 30 authorized Amazon reviewers. In Seller Central, an early reviewer program is available to products that have no or few reviews. It encourages customers who've purchased your product to share their true experience, though you won't know whether those will result in a positive or negative review.

Another way to generate reviews for your brand is to announce your presence on Amazon to your social media followers and encourage them to "tell others what you think of us." Of course, this is no guarantee of a positive review. And here's a word of warning: do not use language that in any way attempts to influence the reviewer!

There are also agencies that specialize in review programs, but do your research to make sure they're reputable. Amazon doesn't suffer fools lightly and has removed thousands of what they believed were fake reviews. *TechCrunch* reports (Conger, 2016) that since early 2015, Amazon has sued more than 1,000 reviewers who posted fake reviews for cash. So yes, there are consequences.

YOUR REVIEW STRATEGY: A CHECKLIST

1. **Fully Leverage Content**

   Your content is your single greatest asset for selling online. Use every opportunity you have to put your best brand foot forward—title, images, video, bullet points, product description, enhanced or A+ content, and finally, by inspiring and engaging with truthful, thoughtful reviews.

2. **Provide Consistently Positive Experience**

   Provide a consistently exceptional experience with your product and fulfillment, and with any customer service issues that arise

3. **Respond Proactively**

   Mitigate negative feedback with proactive education that includes helpful hints for using your products, as well as by offering ways that known issues can be rectified before the customer contacts Amazon or leaves negative feedback. Always keep your responses positive and engaging.

4. **Monitor Feedback**

   Monitor your reviews regularly for opportunities to
   improve your offerings or service. Know that in some
   cases with FBA sellers, through the support portal,
   you can request to have negative product reviews
   removed if they are actually fulfillment complaints
   caused by Amazon and not a true evaluation of
   your product.

5. **Never Manipulate or Compensate**

   Do *not* under any circumstances attempt to manipulate reviews through compensation, other incentives,
   or invalid removal requests. This is one of the few
   areas where you can attempt to manipulate a key
   factor of your success, and Amazon is increasingly
   policing and penalizing such activity, as we mentioned in our two real-life examples.

6. **Repeat Consistently**

   Continue your review generation activities indefi-
   nitely. Amazon's review algorithm does eventually
   discount older reviews and weights newer reviews
   more heavily.

Through its review program, Amazon has provided you
with a means to gain valuable feedback and validate your
product concept in order to improve and meet or exceed

customer needs. Don't discount reviewer comments with "They don't know what they're talking about," because this is where you can hear the honest feedback that your husband or employee may not freely share. We've seen brand managers bristle at reviews they didn't particularly care for when instead they should have used the information as a gift. And we've seen extremely successful brands treat this info as informal panel data they would've had to pay a fortune for in market research. The choice is yours!

OTHER RANKING FACTORS

Here are a few other critical components that determine where and how high you rank for searches on Amazon.

- **Price**

    While we have encouraged you to ensure profitability with your pricing strategy, it is important to understand that with all other things being equal, customers will purchase a product from the seller or platform that has the lowest price. Or they may purchase a similar product from a brand that has the lowest price. Amazon knows this, so your selling price has potential impact on your placement. (Though, if your product sells better than other products for other reasons, this factor will be mitigated.)

    In addition, if you compete at all with other sellers in your listing, you will not win the Buy Box if your price is higher. This underscores the importance of managing your pricing strategy in the total marketplace so that you do not create a situation where a 3P seller is able to purchase your product at a price that competes with your own pricing on Amazon.

- **Availability (In-stock Ratio)**

  Your in-stock rate is a direct factor in your Amazon ranking; it's also an indirect factor, because by definition, your sales velocity will decline if customers are unable to purchase your product for a period of time.

  This leads to an important rule: **do not stock out on Amazon.**

  Sometimes unavoidable circumstances in your business force you to be out of inventory, but take every precaution possible to keep enough stock on-hand to sell uninterruptedly. Don't overdo it, though, or you'll incur unnecessary storage fees. It's a fine line you must walk. Luckily, Amazon provides helpful, fairly accurate forecasting of estimated stock-out dates for each product, based on inventory available and current sales velocities.

- **Fulfillment Method**

  Providing a seamless customer experience is essential to your success on Amazon and is also a factor in the ranking algorithm. Selling to (vendor) or through

(FBA) Amazon are your best options, because on these platforms you will be eligible for the coveted Prime badge, which also increases conversion among customers.

There's also now a Merchant Fulfilled Prime designation, for brands that self-fulfill their product (often perishable brands), but this evolving program has fairly rigorous standards that may be tough to maintain in the long run.

The bottom line is that you have the highest chance of success with the Prime badge and fulfillment that meets the high expectation of Amazon shoppers.

- **Promotions**

  The promotional functionality Amazon offers is constantly evolving (more about those opportunities in Chapter 9). Coupons and other promotions we will cover can have some positive impact on the presence and conversion of your products on Amazon.

Since the purpose of this book is to provide the core framework for your business's success on Amazon, we're focusing on the most important elements that are unlikely to change substantially over time. There are other current supporting details that change more frequently; these can be found online or through our own real-time presentations and writings.

YOUR REWARDS FOR GETTING THIS RIGHT

RANKINGS FOR RELEVANT KEYWORDS

Like Google, Amazon is a search engine, which means that for any given search phrase, the engine determines which listings should appear and in what order. They just have a different set of factors to make those determinations, since Google evolved primarily to rank *information* and Amazon ranks *products*. Both use proprietary algorithms. Google's initial algorithm was based on links from other websites, though it's become more complex over the years. Amazon's algorithm is based on factors that are much more concrete and harder to manipulate, because it is primarily based on actual customer transactions.

PRODUCT SUGGESTIONS

Just below the imagery and brief description on each Amazon product detail page are product suggestion pods, variations of Frequently Bought Together and Also Recommended, features where Amazon shows similar products to the one on the listing page. These are determined by Amazon's view-and-purchase algorithms. Again, the products shown in these pods are determined by actual customer purchase behavior. As these placements are earned for similar, related, or competing products, Amazon will generate significantly more traffic for you for free. This is known as your "earned media" on Amazon.

Amazon's goal is to satisfy each customer's needs and to help them purchase as much and as often as possible. They do this by surfacing products that might be relevant to the customer, in a variety of means and through a variety of popularity and matching algorithms.

MISSION-DRIVEN SUCCESS

Little did Phil Hughes know when he joined the Peace Corps in 2003 that 10 years later, he'd be an entrepreneur. As a community health volunteer in Kenya, Phil lived in a tiny village with no running water and no electricity, working to educate the community about HIV/AIDS.

Though more of a numbers and economics guy, he started to question the poverty that was pervasive in this part of the world. There were virtually no jobs in rural Africa, so he started to think about the well-practiced "ground up development" philosophy of the Peace Corps, and how he could help this community make money to send their kids to school or further invest in the growth of their farms.

In 2011, after earning an MBA in international business, Phil returned to Africa, this time to Rwanda to work with coffee farmers. The combined expertise of his MBA and over four years working with African farmers led Phil to build a business grounded in a mission. The idea was to dry fruit, an asset that was already grown on their farms, and develop it into a commercial product for the US market. Rural farmers had mangos and bananas galore, but couldn't sell them all or transport them to a bigger market from their distant location. So much of this fruit would rot on the ground: not just wasted food, but wasted income.

And that's how Mavuno Harvest was founded. The company now offers nine different fruit and nut products, all sourced from small-scale farmers in Uganda, Kenya, Burkina Faso, Ghana, and Côte d'Ivoire. It's also getting money into these communities, not through charity but through hard work.

Fast forward to 2013, when Mavuno Harvest was exhibiting at the Fancy Food Show. A representative from Amazon came to their booth and urged Phil to launch Mavuno Harvest on Amazon…so they did. And Phil had the same experience as many other brands.

"We started selling on Amazon in 2013, but we weren't putting much effort into Amazon because I didn't understand it and didn't have the time to learn it." This is the point where some brands get discouraged, but Phil sought outside help by working with an Amazon-specific broker.

"When we started working with [our Amazon agency] in 2016, our business really took off. They understand SEO (search engine optimization) and advertising, and how to spend our dollars effectively. From there, our business just skyrocketed. Our first order, after we invested in the broker, was more than we'd sold on Amazon the entire previous year."

Mavuno Harvest is also in retail stores and all the major distributors, but Amazon is definitely their fastest-growing channel. We agree with Phil when he says, "It's just insane how fast buying food online has exploded, and it is just going to keep going mainstream. It gives us a really good opportunity to explain our brand and tell our story. And it's a great marketing tool for small brands that don't necessarily have huge marketing budgets. A cool, fast, effective way to market. We're not the first dried fruit to be invented, so it's important to get eyeballs on our product so we can tell our story. We just want to be the dried mango you see first."

We asked Phil how Amazon helps his mission-driven company fulfill its vision. "The mission is to increase income for small farmers in Africa and avoid food waste. How do we do that? The easy answer is we need to sell these products. How do we sell these products? By telling our story and getting our product in front of people's eyes. Amazon is probably the easiest channel [we can use] to do both of those things. When you are in a store and looking for dried mango, maybe you pick ours or maybe you pick someone else's. You can pick up the bag and read the story, or you can go to the website to learn more later, but those are all extra steps. You want to make it as simple and fast as possible for the consumer, and Amazon makes that possible."

Every brand has its own unique take on Amazon. Some value the geographic reach and instant national distribution. Some value the autonomy of determining their own outcomes. And there is the rare company, like Mavuno Harvest, who knows that when Amazon helps them to sell more product, they can do more good.

NAVIGATE

9

—◦◦◦—

DRIVING TRAFFIC & SALES

There's no "build it and they will come" on Amazon. Just as you can't sit in your idle car at Point A and wish yourself to Point B, you have to have intelligent traffic acquisition in any eComm strategy to get where you want to go.

Of course, brick-and-mortar placements require marketing strategies, too! But placement in physical stores comes with at least *some* existing foot traffic. For example, if your product is in the dairy case in your local supermarket, people who wander by or shop that department will see it there. Whether they buy it is another story, one that involves things like packaging, price point, brand recognition, and how compelling are the competing products. But on that shelf, at least, you're in the game.

Online, placements are much easier to acquire—you could go live on Amazon or a website in a day. But that doesn't mean you've actually achieved anything in terms of introducing people to your product. In fact, in most cases, new online content exists in the ether alone and unnoticed. This is a hard concept for some to understand, particularly when they come from the traditional retail world. Don't get us wrong, *content is the foundation of your brand success* and the underpinning of your marketing campaigns. But it exists in a vacuum if you don't get eyes on your brand, and that's where effective marketing comes into play.

PAY TO PLAY

If you're unfamiliar with eComm and online traffic acquisition, the idea of paying for placements can be difficult to stomach. But in most cases, and especially for newer brands and products, investing in initial momentum is critical to both your early success and longer-term growth trajectory.

Also, the need for paid media never goes away, and even increases over time. The reason is simple: most online platforms, from Google to Facebook to Amazon, start as mostly or entirely free services to grow and acquire larger user bases. But once a certain critical mass is achieved, they start monetizing their audience by offering advertising solutions, surfacing the valuable user data they are gathering, and requiring payment to access it.

So what was once a free placement is now pushed down the search results page or to some other more peripheral position by a new paid placement. And as paid placements become more numerous and prominent, they monopolize the majority of the most viewed and valuable real estate on the page. If you're early to a platform, or in a less competitive industry or niche, enjoy your toll-free traffic while you can, because it won't last long. In most cases, when you don't invest at all in paid media, you're leaving a big chunk of growth and opportunity on the table for your competitors.

Earned Media on Amazon

Along with search rankings, Amazon's recommendation engine is one of the largest potential drivers of traffic to your product. And as with your search rankings, your ability to rank in these recommendation pods is influenced by sales velocity, combined with how your product is viewed and purchased relative to other products. The more of these interactions and the better the conversion rates, the more likely Amazon is to suggest your product alongside the others that customers are viewing. This is why you should consider your paid media as an investment in additional "free" presence in the future.

Driving Initial Traffic with Amazon Marketing Tools

Amazon provides a number of highly effective promotional tools directly within the platform that can help you drive sales velocity and reach portions of their vast customer base with relative ease, as well as provide end-to-end measurement from click to sale. These are evolving at such breakneck speed, with such a plethora of options, they can be difficult to navigate and prioritize. Here's a quick overview.

Sponsored Products

This is Amazon's pay-per-click (PPC) offering, allowing you to display the products you select for the search terms you think are most relevant to the customers searching for your product or category. Over time, you'll be able to gather comprehensive data on how customers are interacting with these ads, which products convert the best, your average cost per acquisition, and search terms driving sales that you would never have originated on your own. (The results can be truly surprising!)

The key here is that these pay-to-play campaigns allow you to garner *immediate* placement for relevant search terms that would otherwise take a lot of time to generate organically (if the rankings can be acquired at all), and begin to drive sales velocity that will ultimately help you earn placements organically to further drive your business.

Your initial strategy should be to:

- Optimize your listings as comprehensively as possible. (This will evolve over time as you gather the aforementioned data.)
- Set up an automated campaign with the products most likely to be the entry points to your product line (such as variety packs or smaller pack sizes with lower price points, in most cases). Set an initial

bid to start gathering search query data that can be accessed through Amazon's Advertising Reports section.

- Create additional manually-targeted campaigns with specific, relevant keywords, with higher average bids than your automated campaign (if you feel you have enough knowledge of the advertising platform.)

From here, you'll gather data to optimize bids and to migrate converting keywords from your automated campaign to your manual ones.

Creating and managing PPC campaigns is a fairly specialized skill set that can be time-intensive, particularly in the first few months or year. If you don't have the experience or time to learn the strategies and do the manual management yourself, we strongly recommend hiring a skilled employee or agency to manage your campaigns for you (we offer such services).

SPONSORED BRANDS

A newer advertising placement relative to Sponsored Products, Sponsored Brands appear at the very top of search results pages (and are starting to show up elsewhere as well), in a banner format that generally displays your logo, a title you provide, and a chosen selection of your products.

This ad format requires more aggressive bids, since only one ad shows at a time and the placement is quite prominent. But it's also great for both branding and direct response and can be quite effective for converting potential customers. The beauty of this tactic is that even if consumers don't click the ad to reach your product page, this banner provides exposure and gets new eyes on your brand. And remember, you only pay when someone clicks on the ad.

Sponsored Brands require you to apply for Brand Registry, and traffic generally converts better when sent to your Storefront, which also requires an approved brand registration.

There are a few additional marketing programs available on the vendor side, though again, most of the important ones are being brought over to the seller side, and we expect this trend to continue.

AMAZON MEDIA GROUP

Amazon has an absolute treasure trove of some of the most valuable data available anywhere, and a proprietary set of data at that. While Google knows the themes and patterns of your search history (indicating intent and interests for example), Amazon has irrefutable data on *what each customer has actually purchased* with their hard-earned money.

Imagine the most fervent purchasers and early adopters of shopping on Amazon—maybe you're one yourself—and then imagine how much Amazon can infer from their purchase behavior. Now add the fact that nearly half of all eComm activity takes place directly on Amazon, and imagine the immensity and value of that information.

Amazon Media Group (AMG) is a rapidly evolving display media platform that seeks to surface this data for businesses to advertise against.

Information from higher to lower purchase intent in the buying cycle includes consumers who have one or more of these purchasing patterns:

- Are "in market" for your product category, inferred from recent behavior
- Have purchased in your product's category
- Viewed or purchased a competitor's product
- Viewed your products but did not purchase
- Purchased your product in the past

All of these segments and more are visible and available through AMG. Standard display ad sizes are the main creative, though unique placements are also available (such as Kindle Fire tablet devices).

The minimums to advertise via AMG are high (currently upward of $25,000 per month), so the platform is really only viable for larger businesses. However, as the program matures, it's likely to become more available through a mostly self-serve portal similar to Amazon's other marketing programs.

DRIVING TRAFFIC WITH AMAZON MARKETING TOOLS

Amazon has added many new promotional tools within Seller Central (such as Giveaways and Buy One Get One), and will surely continue to add other promotions. However, not all are created equal. So here's a look at some of the core promotional tools that drive sales velocity for your products.

LIGHTNING DEALS

Once available to only high-volume sellers with access to an Amazon representative, Amazon has released self-serve Lightning Deal functionality to sellers within the dashboard. However, Amazon algorithmically determines if and when your products are eligible on a weekly basis.

Lightning Deals require at least a 20% discount off your *recent* lowest price and must run for at least four hours, with presence on Amazon Deals, one of the most highly trafficked pages on the site. They are a phenomenal way to increase your sales velocity, especially as a newly launched brand, and we recommend leveraging them regularly in your first year or two. Lightning Deals are also great when introducing a new product to your existing line, to get buyers who will also, hopefully, review your product.

The only downside is that buyers who are primarily deal seekers may be lower-value customers, less likely to repeat purchase. Still, these deals are a great way to drive product trial, reviews, and sales that ultimately contribute to your product ranking.

COUPONS

Amazon does provide the ability to create coupon codes for your customers, similar to your own eComm platform. However, these are "clippable" coupons that display on your product detail page (the customer must see and select the coupon option), and there's a cost associated with each "clip," so you'll have to set a budget for that fee (plus the discounted amount). Coupons can offer incentive for your potential consumer to purchase within a short time frame, increasing your conversion rates. Using a one-time-use coupon to acquire new buyers is an excellent strategy in conjunction with your ad campaign.

DRIVING TRAFFIC *TO* AMAZON

To this point, we've discussed leveraging the functionality within Amazon's platform to drive your business, and this is critical. However, often one of the best ways to create success *on* Amazon is via success *outside of* Amazon.

External promotions, partnerships, public relations campaigns, social media influencers—acquiring these placements can have massive impact on your business and catapult your sales velocity beyond your competitors. How exactly to formulate and execute on these strategies varies widely by category and brand. It will require consistent effort over time, and usually an investment, unless you have an incredibly unique brand or product that compels others to tell your story for free. And early on, this effort will often be from the founder, perhaps eventually moving to an agency or to in-house employee(s).

You should also consider driving traffic from other non-Amazon marketing channels such as Google, Facebook, Pinterest, and others which can help drive your critical sales velocity. But there's a tradeoff in promoting Amazon over your own website: when a sale takes place on Amazon, *they* own the customer data and control your ability to communicate. So while you may have the initial revenue, you lose the business value of owning the data, along with the ability to communicate with that customer as you please.

In Chapter 12, we review Amazon's offering from late 2017, which allows you to create a self-contained website directly on Amazon.com as well as track third-party traffic sources to these pages.

10

DATA & ANALYTICS

W hen they explore Amazon's data offerings, people from the traditional retail world or with expertise in online analytics usually have the same reaction: frustration and confusion.

Despite Amazon being the world's largest online retailer, not to mention an impressive technology enterprise that hosts the infrastructure of some of the largest companies in the world, the retail analytics back end is mostly a home-grown platform, a Frankenstein's monster-like amalgamation of years of iterative growth and change. And both its seller and vendor reporting reflects this. A Vendor Manager once described Amazon's analytics as "built by PhDs, for PhDs," which is why an entire industry has been built around taking this raw data and turning it into a map for actionable insights.

If you're accustomed to robust analytics from either your eComm platform or Google Analytics, you may be befuddled and/or frustrated by Amazon's offerings. And though Amazon is quickly becoming one of the largest advertising platforms, its analytics capabilities are still evolving and catching up in many ways. Frankly, if you're used to platforms like Google and Facebook, you'll be underwhelmed by Amazon's data capabilities (though to be fair, they're changing quickly).

Add in the fact that you don't own the customer data for your Amazon.com transactions and how Amazon works to restrict your access to that data as much as possible to protect their business, and it's easy to see how you might feel like you're driving in the dark.

There are third-party services that augment data analysis capabilities, and many companies choose to work with those. Let's shine a light on what's directly available in Amazon's interfaces so you can see what you're working with and what makes the most sense for you.

VENDOR CENTRAL

Amazon offers a dashboard called Amazon Retail Analytics (ARA) Basic, which provides fundamental sales data by day, week, month, quarter, and year. It unquestionably has its limitations. For example, you can only get monthly sales by item for the most recent month. So if the most current reporting month is May and you want to see April, you've missed your chance. If you want by-item, by-month historical data, you have to harvest the Amazon data monthly and build your own dashboard to get a detailed historical snapshot. A second set of reports provides a variety of metrics on operational performance.

If you want to dig more deeply, Amazon offers ARA Premium for a negotiated fee, typically a percentage of sales for larger brands. This data is decidedly more robust, but you may need some help making heads or tails out of it and translating it into information that's usable for building strategy. This is where outside firms—often made up of former Amazon pros—can help. They know how to crunch that data and advise you on your specific business needs.

And the competitive information that brands are accustomed to receiving from SPINS, Nielsen, and IRI? It's simply not available in eComm. So while you can get more detailed information about your brand from ARA Premium, you will not have insight about the category and your competitors. Amazon has been very discreet about sharing data from the very beginning, and though it sounds counterintuitive, in some ways, that can be a huge advantage to new and small brands.

First of all, without this exposure, they don't have the big CPG companies seeing them as a threat to their business and using their powers to crush them. This allows smaller, newer brands to safely fly under the radar while building their business.

Secondly, even if that level of detail were available on Amazon, small brands couldn't afford to buy it, so it would really only serve the interests of the biggest brands. And that of course would upend the equi-system that Amazon has so carefully built.

Third, lack of data prevents smaller brands from limiting their aspirations. Is it really useful for a new and innovative laundry detergent company to know how much business Tide is doing on Amazon? Or is it better to work hard and trust that they'll excel in that very cool niche, with a brand that really has nothing to do with the big conventionals? No category is mature online, so the sky's the limit when it comes to assessing your relative opportunity and seizing it.

Other areas of analytics worth checking out are reports on the success of your Amazon coupons and Amazon Advertising campaigns. Amazon offers a keyword report that provides sales and performance metrics for Sponsored Products and Sponsored Brands. There's also reporting on ASIN sales for Sponsored Product campaigns, as well as reports that detail actual search terms entered by shoppers that resulted in a click on your Sponsored Product promotion.

Finally, Amazon provides a report that details your results by the ASINs included in campaigns versus those not included. Amazon is actively expanding the reporting capabilities on this portal, because they realize that when brands see results, they'll spend more on these marketing activities. In this case, transparency does have its benefits, for both the brand and Amazon.

Seller Central

Analytics

Most day-to-day analytics are found in the Business Reports section. Here you'll find familiar metrics (with slightly unfamiliar Amazon-specific names) like sessions, orders, revenue, and other data points that can be viewed daily, weekly, or monthly.

You'll also be able to view similar metrics separated out by product, as well as the quantity and quality of customer reviews received for each. You'll find Buy Box percentage in total and by product, which allows you to determine how often you're winning the all-important Buy Box on Amazon (being featured as the primary seller). As a retailer, you'll be competing with all other retailers who sell a given product, while as a brand, you'll be competing against your distribution partners and retailers, and quite likely resellers as well.

Finally, you'll be able to view your Amazon metrics, such as positive and negative feedback received based on your fulfillment and customer interactions.

Conspicuously absent from all of this is any data about the customers themselves. Unlike with your own eComm platform, you won't be able to see data on things like repeat customers versus new ones or other types of browsing activity that could guide your strategy on your own website.

Inventory

There are several inventory-related selections within the Amazon Selling Coach reporting section, and the most useful one is inventory planning. Amazon will actually calculate your recent sales velocity at the product level and provide estimated remaining days of inventory to assist you in production planning and/or new inventory shipments.

Since staying in stock is crucial to maintaining your sales velocity and product rankings, you can see why this is extremely important.

Fulfillment

If you're using Amazon FBA to store and fulfill inventory, you'll have access to this section on fulfillment. It contains a vast selection of reporting, with information on the following:

- Your inventory quantities, health, history, and removals
- All order information, including names and addresses
- Subscribe & Save revenue
- Storage fees
- Return information

A word of caution: be sure to carefully review Amazon's extremely restrictive policies regarding the customer information provided. As a general rule, this information cannot be used for marketing, particularly for promoting anything outside of Amazon, like your website. Yes, they're your orders, but they're Amazon's customers.

Advertising

Compared to Google, Facebook, and other established media platforms, Amazon's actionable reporting on your advertising spend leaves a lot to be desired.

But within Campaign Manager, you'll have access to performance at the keyword level, which is essential for optimizing your advertising spend on Amazon, as well as performance for the SKUs you've selected in each keyword group.

You'll also be able to pull Search Query level reporting for your broader keyword targeting within the Advertising Reports selection, so that you can isolate poorly performing or irrelevant queries to exclude them from your advertising with negative keywords.

But you won't have much else. As of this writing, Amazon doesn't provide any additional segmentation such as data by device, location, audience, or any other advertising segment you might find useful on other platforms. We hope that the transparency of ad spending on Amazon will increase as the platform evolves.

Other

Financial reports, such as a history of payments from Amazon and documents needed for tax purposes, are available in their respective categories in the Reports menu.

11

HOW TO STRUCTURE YOUR
TEAM FOR AMAZON

For those new to eComm, it may come as a surprise that core mental and structural changes may be required to effectively manage this business. This is another reason why so many small and new companies are so successful on Amazon: they get this new model and are nimble at adapting to it. Actually, in many cases, it doesn't even require adapting, since this is the way these newer brands are coming to market—they're essentially eComm natives. Also, with small companies, the assignment of roles is usually not as rigid, so all three of the company employees can jump in and do whatever needs to be done.

If you don't fall into either the small or adaptable category, knowing the best practices for organizational structure in this channel and how to guide new company thinking can make an enormous difference.

And like every other important cultural shift, it starts at the top. If the CEO isn't behind the Amazon initiative, it will probably fail, because without a cohesive commitment from leaders in all departments who are helping to drive the strategy, you as the sole Amazon cheerleader will be going it alone.

Why, you might ask, wouldn't leadership get behind this tectonic shift in retail? Here are the top four reasons we've heard, over and over again:

1. Our products aren't the type that sell online.
2. We haven't decided that this is the direction we want to go as a company.
3. It's such a small piece of our business, it doesn't make sense to devote the resources.
4. Our distributors/retailers have asked us not to sell on Amazon.

Let's break these down for you, one by one.

1. Our products aren't the type that sell online.

There just *aren't* many products that "don't sell online." Kitchen sinks sell online. Frozen pizza crusts sell online. Luxury beauty items sell online. Food-service products, sporting gear, water, chocolate, laundry detergent, jewelry, hair extensions, mattresses…they all sell online. We could go on and on, but you get the idea. Here's a challenge: find us an item that doesn't sell online. We'll wait.

THIS PRODUCT SELLS ONLINE

We caught up with Kevin McCarthy, CEO of UNREAL Chocolate, to find out how the first year of selling on Amazon was going in one of the toughest categories online: chocolate. Not tough because consumers aren't buying; they are buying in abundance. Tough because even with the best precautions, chocolate could arrive on your doorstep completely melted.

In fact, Amazon does not ship chocolate (or other meltable products) between April 1 and October 1, in order to minimize a predictably poor customer experience. But that doesn't entirely solve for the fragility of temperature-sensitive products in regions like the southern US, where it can be 90 degrees in December. And when you're a natural brand that doesn't contain preservatives and other ingredients that help traditional brands keep "fresh," it's even harder.

Still, Amazon is where the greatest opportunity exists for a brand like UNREAL, whose chocolate-loving customers are seeking natural, better-for-you options to traditional snacks and are avid online shoppers. As Kevin aptly put it, "We see it as the greatest opportunity for our brand and one of our greatest challenges. With the rapid shifts in consumer purchasing behavior that will continue to shift, it is something that is really important to us. Regardless of it being a bit difficult, not diving in at Amazon was not an option. It is not only a growth opportunity, but also where we engage with our customer." And opportunities are expanding with Prime Now, Fresh, and Amazon Go.

When UNREAL launched in October 2017, just in time for Halloween, they had a huge first month with Amazon. "It is impossible to make a sales forecast for Amazon when you're launching, and we were pleasantly surprised," Kevin says.

But then UNREAL ran into some snags and had to quickly troubleshoot on the supply-chain side of the business—needing to understand conditions in Amazon's warehouses to determine where problems can occur. Was it the trucking into the fulfillment center, the temperature there, or during delivery to consumer? As Kevin notes, "There is no way to test on Amazon without going live with your products and figuring it out."

This research led to two best practices. First, keeping product in Amazon's fulfillment centers for the shortest time possible—sell quickly and replenish—which, by the way, is best practice for any brand using Amazon's FBA platform. Another smart measure was using the UNREAL community around the country to order product and to help spot problems before the consumer does. "Amazon customers are so used to perfection. They expect that everything is going to be delivered on time and with ease of use. So when it doesn't happen, it doesn't necessarily reflect on Amazon, it reflects on the brand. We would love to have a solution, even an ice pack at an extra cost, but right now that option does not exist at Amazon."

Because of this, Kevin stressed the importance of monitoring and responding to negative reviews, as well as another twist. "When you are 'off' Amazon in the summer months, you're not really off Amazon. There are third-party sellers that are going to continue to sell UNREAL and ship directly to the consumer. You don't know how they are shipping and what the consumer experience is going to be. Even though they are not your listings, you need to be on top of it, because it still reflects on your brand."

By staying involved in the summer and keeping an eye on third-party listings of their brand, they're able to engage with their consumer to change a poor brand experience into a positive one. It's important "that we do everything we can to connect to that customer and make it right."

When we asked Kevin what additional advice he would give to brands that are launching meltable products on Amazon, he answered, "Start small and prove the concept from a delivery point of view. It is easy to fall in love with the vision of being a super successful Amazon brand, but with a temperature-sensitive product, you need to be on top of managing quality. Consider worst-case scenarios and how to handle them. If you don't, you're creating more work for yourself trying to bring those consumers back to your brand."

And that is how to be a successful chocolate brand on Amazon.

2. We haven't decided that this is the direction we want to go as a company.

Well, guess what? The industry has decided for you. Kantar Retail (Retail in Motion Study, 2017) projects that within the next three years, 33% of electronics, 32% of books, 28% of toys, sporting goods, and apparel, and 18% of home goods like furniture will be purchased online. Most relevant to our clients is Nielsen and FMI's $100 billion grocery projection. I don't know about you, but I'd like a piece of that pie.

3. It's such a small piece of our business.

Keep thinking this, and it will absolutely remain a small piece of your business because eComm is the channel driving growth in retail, and as brands that have led in eComm have shown, early in has definite advantages. On the flip side, the longer you wait, the harder it is to break through all the noise, challenge the online category leaders, and build the business you deserve. And what this typically requires is wise investment spending and over-resourcing against the relative size of the business to get the Amazon flywheel moving.

4. Our distributors/retailers have asked us not to sell on Amazon.

When did your distributors and retailers acquire your company? Allowing the self-interest of other companies to drive your business decisions is, we're sorry to say, a losing strategy. Worse news for brands that buy into this position—if you don't determine your brand's destiny on Amazon, others will. The third-party marketplace will take care of that for you, and it may not be in a way that you like.

Third parties can destroy your carefully crafted pricing structure by purchasing your product on promotion from one of your distributors and selling below the optimal price point. They can buy product from Costco, inflate the price, and still be a top seller of your product. They can sell old, out-of-code product, damaged product, and discontinued product, and you won't have control over these actions. They can post the worst possible content or low-quality photos and make claims that are untrue. You might not even be able to track down a physical entity in an attempt to correct these problems, or to convince Amazon to help you with it.

You may ask Amazon to shut down a third-party seller by claiming that they are an unauthorized reseller of your product. But guess what? There's no such thing as an "unauthorized" seller if they're getting your product legitimately. The only time Amazon will intervene on behalf of a brand is when a seller is hocking counterfeit product. And unless you're Nike or a luxury beauty brand, it's highly unlikely this applies to you.

So there you have it!

Now that you and your leadership team have thought things through, we hope you're ready to move forward and learn what the rest of the team needs to know about working with Amazon.

There are quite a few things to know, starting with the challenges involved in setting up your account, listing products, and shipping orders. These can turn into frustrations for various team members and can result in a negative attitude toward the business, which can ultimately derail the whole endeavor.

To go back to the road trip analogy, if you've got a group of people in your car who can't agree on—or don't want to go to—the same route or destination, it makes for a miserable ride. But if your team is all in it together, even when things go wrong, you can share road-warrior stories and mitigate the frustration. So here are a few insights and strategies that can help to get everyone on the same page.

THE TEAM & HOW IT WORKS

Usually, the sales manager responsible for Amazon is the hub of the wheel. And in each function that involves another department—whether marketing, finance, or operations—it's essential that one specific person within that department acts as the Amazon expert and point person. We're not suggesting that this is the employee's entire job; they may only devote 5% of their effort to Amazon. But they are the pro, the expert, the go-to person who knows how to get things done. Having the business touched by a number of customer service people or whomever happens to be free in finance on a particular day ensures that nobody will truly gain proficiency and a comfort level with Amazon. Efforts can be duplicated or even cancel each other out, and small challenges turn into problems or crises.

OPERATIONS

If you're working with Vendor Central, you'll be asked to meet shipping timelines that are typically out of the usual scope: three days from order receipt to get it out the door. Depending on your business, this may also require coordinating shipment from multiple warehouses within this expedited time frame. There are labeling requirements unique to Amazon that your team needs to understand, and there may be glitches in receiving at Amazon's end.

If you're working in Seller Central, you're the one who determines the timing and amount of product to ship into Amazon fulfillment centers. However, once you make that plan, Amazon will tell you what quantities to ship to which locations and provide you with labels that must be applied to each selling unit. You can see how different this is from working with a classic brick-and-mortar retailer and why an Amazon leader with a honed skill set will be a true asset in operations.

Eventually, this person becomes so attuned to what can go right and wrong with Amazon that they anticipate hurdles and challenges before they happen. This role should be filled by a person who has a natural curiosity and is comfortable with constantly shifting waters, because if there was ever one truth about Amazon, it's that change is inevitable.

Customer Service

The operations team's best friend, your customer service pro will be called on not only to provide service to Amazon as they would any other customer, but also to figure out what went wrong with the latest shipment, why Amazon is claiming a shortage on the current order, or why it didn't arrive. And they'll need to resolve all of this by becoming proficient in Amazon's automated vendor and/or seller portals, where they'll file a case when something goes wrong.

There will typically *not* be a live person to call at Amazon to chat through these problems, so the more adept your customer service team becomes at using all the automation that Amazon provides, the more successful you'll be as a brand. Amazon's philosophy is HOTW—hands off the wheel. Understanding and embracing that philosophy lets you expertly put your hands ON the wheel.

Additionally, a customer service person may take on tasks that are not traditionally a part of their job description. For example, because of the dedicated use of Amazon portal automation, setting up new items and filing cases for other departments that need Amazon issues resolved can all be a part of the customer service role.

Marketing

Here's where creativity and flexibility come into play. By now, you've probably guessed that traditional brick-and-mortar marketing tactics don't work online. Paper coupons, free-standing inserts (FSIs), and display materials, to name a few—there's no place for any of them in eComm.

What that means for some companies is that there is no additional specific marketing or dedicated funding for eComm. And because of this, traditional marketing departments may defer Amazon support to a department sometimes called Customer Marketing. This is typically where a small amount of specific funds lives for unique retailer programs outside of normal marketing support. But if you think about it, all marketing for Amazon needs to be "customer-specific," because traditional tactics do not apply.

This distinction can cause great angst for team members in sales, because there's no meaningful additional funding for this unique customer. That's one reason that walls between sales and marketing have been disappearing in recent years. Marketing now understands that they need to view Amazon as a unique animal and provide adequate funding. Even the distinction in funding buckets is disappearing— that is who's responsible for the cost of coupons versus spending on search—is becoming less relevant as companies structure around the need to just get things done. Dedicating a marketing resource to the health and well-being of the eComm business can determine the difference in the success or failure of your Amazon initiative. But the bottom line is, as you have heard from us more than once, without marketing, you have no eComm business.

Brand Marketing/R & D

These two roles are combined because together they're responsible for product innovation and development for the brand. These members of your multifunctional team are essential to ensure that you have the right products in the right packs for success at Amazon. Also, eComm product development must be integrated into the product innovation pipeline and not addressed as an afterthought. Developing the most innovative six-pack of the most life-changing, awe-inspiring spray cleaner in the world is going to be meaningless for one of your sales channels—eComm—if you don't consider all the product factors that will lead to success.

For instance, have you solved for leakage? Is a six-pack the right selling unit, or is that a two-year supply? What about the spray trigger? Will it be intact when it's shipped to the consumer? It's exponentially more efficient to address all of these issues in product development than it is to have to backtrack after the fact and find a quick-fix solution for Amazon. Your Amazon sales lead can often help guide this process, because they've now become the informal Amazon expert in areas they didn't even know about a year ago.

Finance

Because Amazon is a different beast, it's important to have an expert in finance who understands it. In the case of the seller model, finance will be called upon to reconcile payment and statements every two weeks. They'll need to account for inventory that's housed in different locations, as part of what's often internally considered a consignment model. They will be asked to provide documentation when Amazon's Vendor Central in-stock team files a claim for shortages or lost product. And equally important, they'll want to develop an Amazon profit and loss statement to truly understand how customer profitability varies from traditional retailers and dig into optimizing cost to serve.

Another rising-star position with clients is an Amazon coordinator—essentially, a project manager. This person works at the brand's corporate headquarters and takes the lead on resolving complex issues, serving as the in-house expert on all things Amazon, and engaging with the various team members to create the best solutions for the business. They may need to keep a new product process on track or help execute the Amazon marketing plan. A person with this level of expertise to align all the moving pieces is an invaluable addition to the Amazon team.

Remember, this evolution doesn't need to be daunting. Until the scale of your business requires dedicated attention, your Amazon team is a subset of your existing team. They'll still fill a greater role in their given department within the organization, but will also bring a wealth of knowledge and expertise to take your Amazon business to new heights. And once the team is assembled, meeting with this group of new Amazon champions to map your progress and continually move your business forward is extremely rewarding for everyone involved.

12

―――∞∞∞―――

DO YOU EVEN NEED A WEBSITE?

C an you imagine a web presence without a website? Within a year or two, this could be a reality for many brands.

For the record, we recommend that you DO have a website now. And we probably always will. At the very least, you need to own your brand's web address and have key information readily accessible for consumers, investors, and media.

Still, recent developments at Amazon hint that the spotlight may be moving away from your website.

Let's look at why.

BRAND REGISTRY

Amazon has long had a reputation for being unfriendly to a company's brand integrity, because for the most part, they have been. At best, Amazon is neutral to brands; at worst, they're undermining. With issues from inaccurate information on listings to listing hijacking to outright counterfeiting, Amazon keeps brand marketers tossing and turning at night.

While Amazon is still a ruthlessly competitive marketplace, particularly for undifferentiated products and retailers who are subject to price undercutting and the whims of customer feedback, an offshoot is sprouting for brands with unique and value-add offerings.

That offshoot is Amazon Brand Registry, which opens up certain trademark and listing protections as well as marketing opportunities, including the aforementioned Enhanced Brand Content and Sponsored Brands.

Its purpose is to allow manufacturers and brand owners some influence and control over the presentation and accuracy of their Amazon listings. Once a brand's application is approved and the appropriate information is (accurately) supplied, the brand owner will have a much-improved ability to control certain information on the listing pages.

But the control is not complete. Brand Registry doesn't offer exclusivity of listing products, for example. But it does provide some additional measures of control and recourse via Amazon's support system. It is not intended for you as a brand to be able to kick third-party sellers you view as "unauthorized" to sell your product off of Amazon.

STOREFRONT

Here's where things really start to get interesting. With Storefront, Amazon provides the ability for a brand to essentially create a mini-website that lives on Amazon.com with a unique URL and completely customizable content. Amazon provides a wide array of module formats that can be strung together seamlessly, some plug-and-play modules and others that offer more free-form content. Additionally, you can now create entirely separate *pages* with their own themes and content, which can expand your organic reach for searches and other customer navigation via Amazon's web property.

That's right: you can now have a website on Amazon. Thus the question, "Do you even need a website anymore?" It will be very interesting to see how this functionality evolves over the coming months and years.

The content and keywords used on product-listing pages were always important and necessary-but-not-sufficient components of any Amazon strategy. But now, even more elements can be optimized to garner customer search traffic for your products.

OFF-AMAZON TRACKING AND ANALYTICS

Many have lamented the complete lack of insight into the outcomes of visitor traffic sent to the Amazon.com property, which is essentially a black hole for data and customer analysis. Conversely, on a brand's own website, there is a full suite of data (via Google Analytics or other platforms) and even likely various customer data via the website's backend platform.

Amazon's offering allows the use of link tagging, with which Amazon can record information about the traffic source and campaign details for later analysis, similar to existing analytics programs. Of course, the data is nowhere near as robust as Google Analytics, but it will surely become more so in the coming months and years. With this new offering, the writing is on the wall: by creating more visibility into performance, Amazon is making a clear and aggressive play toward capturing more off-Amazon traffic.

PIXELING

Though not officially announced, AMG is beginning to offer a website pixel similar to those provided by Google, Facebook, and other ad platforms, to track actions like home-page visits and order completion that take place on your own website (outside of Amazon).

The stated purpose is for audience exclusions with AMG advertising. But once this data is being regularly recorded, what's to stop Amazon from offering all kinds of additional functionality, like targeting these visitors on Amazon, tracking the interplay between website and Amazon traffic, and countless other potential use cases? And why wouldn't you, as a brand, want some of this functionality?

When you combine the impact of an almost fully functional website directly on the Amazon platform with an expanding suite of traffic analytics, it only takes a little imagination to see that Amazon is moving into the domain of a hosted web presence. And it may not be long before a regularly maintained presence *on* Amazon is as important an initiative for brands as their websites are now. Maybe even more so for many brands.

POINTS OF
INTEREST

13

THE NUTPODS STORY: LEVERAGING AMAZON SUCCESS INTO RETAIL

Nutpods is a spectacular example of entrepreneurial success that started with a problem and a dream, which led to massive adoption on Amazon and was then leveraged into the world of traditional retail. In other words, it's a poster child for the new paradigm profiled in this book.

In early 2013, after struggling with pregnancy-induced diabetes and becoming utterly frustrated with the lack of truly healthy nondairy coffee creamer options, Madeline Haydon, the CEO and founder of nutpods, resolved to experiment with her own recipe for a dairy-free, unsweetened creamer with all-natural ingredients.

Roughly six months later, she launched a Kickstarter campaign and raised $32,000 from strangers to pursue her goal. About a year and a half later, Madeline shipped her new formula to Amazon for nutpods' online debut, choosing Amazon as an initial sales channel so Kickstarter backers had a place to reorder.

The reception was everything she'd hoped it would be; the product was well-received as the deliciously creamy alternative to half-and-half that many increasingly health conscious consumers had long awaited. As sales began to increase, the positive reviews soon followed, and the Amazon flywheel began to turn. (Yes, crowdfunding sites can be a great way to jump-start your sales velocity!)

A few years later, nutpods products, which now include three core flavors and multiple seasonal flavors, are well represented in the top 100 grocery SKUs on Amazon, with numerous new flavor launches reaching the top release in the nondairy coffee creamers category. Their most popular limited time seasonal offering, Pumpkin Spice, reached the #1 grocery product on all of Amazon during its run time in 2018!

Nutpods used a combination of paid media channels (such as Sponsored Products and Google AdWords), Amazon's promotional tools (such as Lightning Deals and Enhanced Brand Content), strategic partnerships and influencer outreach, trade shows, and plenty of hustle to steadily grow sales on Amazon and eventually achieve many organic rankings for relevant search terms that further increased sales. Nutpods' success is derived from a combination of a superior product and intelligent use of the marketing tools available.

The importance of a quality product that generated genuine, consistently positive reviews cannot be overstated. You can't fake quality, especially over time as the landscape becomes more competitive.

"Don't underestimate the value of reviews," said Haydon. "Whether or not the consumer ends up buying your product on Amazon or in another channel, most consumers will jump on Amazon to read the reviews of your product, and that social proof is the new way today's consumers are buying. First, consumers want to know companies care about their feedback. So responding to reviews (even the critical or negative ones) shows you're listening to them. It's an indication of the level of service you'll give to your customers, and it's part of your brand experience.

"Second, reviews give you as the brand owner immediate data points for your product. Are the flavors what you want them to be? Is the packaging working for the customer? Is the price point in line with what your consumers want to pay? Are you sufficiently conveying your unique selling proposition? And third, when you raise money, as most of us will, investors will read these same reviews to help determine the strength of your brand."

Though the team deliberated on this point many times over the years, nutpods also chose to launch on Seller Central and remain there exclusively, without ever becoming a vendor or adopting the hybrid model (using vendor and seller simultaneously), which was the prevailing wisdom at the time.

Initially, Seller Central didn't offer the same features as the vendor platform as it now does. For example, Lightning Deals were not available on the seller platform without direct access to a representative (which small companies don't have), Sponsored Brands didn't exist, Enhanced Brand Content was just being released, and other promotional tools either didn't exist at all or only existed on the vendor side. But those are now standard on the seller platform, and the offerings are regularly increased and improved.

Seller Central provided faster payment terms, Net 15 rather than Net 60 days on the vendor side, which was critical for a small, growing business. Seller Central is also "a channel where you can do nimble and nuanced price testing, versus retailers and distributors that require ninety days' notice for pricing changes," said Madeline, as opposed to the vendor side where the brand has no pricing control.

Nutpods also experienced substantial growth after they partnered with a nutritional organization with a large following that fit with their core consumer base. This is a great reminder that some of your best opportunities to drive sales on Amazon might be outside of Amazon.

"Influencers who are sincerely behind your product will legitimize the brand and expose it to relevant audiences," says Madeline. The company consistently tested placement and promotional opportunities with relevant social media influencers, popular bloggers, and nutritional organizations.

Some placements were paid, others earned from previous promotional activity, and certainly not all campaigns were successful, but the overall effort was. After all, a sale is a sale. It makes no difference to the algorithm where the sale originated, and in fact, Amazon encourages all sorts of external traffic generation to their website through various programs.

Madeline also emphasized that you do not necessarily need a big, expensive engagement with an Amazon broker. Much was gleaned via learning and experimentation, though various consultants and in-house team members that played key roles.

Like any other channel, Amazon is not without its challenges. Madeline remembers inventory levels as one of the largest initial struggles. "As a new brand it's difficult to anticipate demand. We stocked out several times in our first year with Amazon because we had such wonderful market reception and weren't able to add production dates or, in some cases, move up our production dates. As a start-up company with limited capital, we had the unavoidable challenge of trying to forecast demand while not producing too much inventory."

This challenge is not unique to Amazon, but being based on recent sales velocity, the algorithm is somewhat punitive to stock-out situations, since there can be no velocity during periods where there's no product for sale. This is why forecasting and ensuring consistently healthy inventory levels is a foundational element of your Amazon business.

Over time, Subscribe & Save became an important component of the business and a reflection of consumer loyalty. It now represents a significant portion of nutpods' Amazon revenue. Most importantly, it is predictable, recurring revenue that can be relied upon, and the company has calculated that subscribers are worth measurably more than other returning customers. Any product that remotely lends itself to repeat usage should offer the subscription option whenever possible—though keep in mind the tiered discounts that Amazon offers to customers; they are funded by the seller and impact profit margins.

After a few years of steadily increasing revenue on Amazon, nutpods has now been able to leverage this success to acquire nationwide distribution with multiple major retailers, including Kroger and Whole Foods, along with myriad specialized natural food stores across the nation. While revenue was almost exclusively on Amazon for the first three to four years, the business is now split between online and offline, with continued growth expected from the retail channel.

However, this never would have been possible without the initial success on Amazon; in fact, the company never would have been able to stay in business by relying on timely and profitable retail placements early on—not by a long shot! Besides the actual Amazon revenue, the sales volume, location data, and customer reviews were critical components in raising capital and securing retail placements.

Nutpods is on the forefront of a nascent digital transition in the grocery industry, which has already disrupted so many other retail industries, and the company is a shining example of a new paradigm, where a brand can be built much more quickly with direct-to-consumer online distribution that leverages that success into the slow-moving, expensive world of traditional retail.

14

—∽৩/৩∾—

OTHER BURNING
QUESTIONS

WHAT ABOUT WHOLE FOODS, AMAZON AND THE FUTURE OF GROCERY?

When Whole Foods Market was acquired in 2017, there was universal shock across the grocery retail industry and beyond. To some, like Tim Sperry, longtime Whole Foods Market executive-turned-consultant, it was hard on the heart. But from a business perspective, it made total sense.

"Whole Foods either had to continue to make acquisitions and morph into something else or be acquired and morph into something else. Whole Foods was not a failed company, it was just not meeting the expectations of Wall Street," Tim said.

Inevitably, in our economy, that's enough to force major change. And, in this case, they may have just gotten a big break. As Tim added, "Given where retail is going, who better to partner up than these two?"

Here are our other questions, Tim's answers, and our parenthetical notes.

B & P: Why Whole Foods and not one of the other grocery chains?

TS: First, Whole Foods was not broken, and Amazon got great real estate, a really good supply chain, and access to some of the best customers in the world. So any other challenges were basically nothing.

(And all for $13 billion, a pretty small chuck of change for Amazon.)

B & P: Why retail at all?

TS: They knew that the entire world was not going to go online. They made that clear by opening up their brick-and-mortar bookstores and Amazon Go stores. They recognized that a large percentage of the retail experience was still going to be done in a facility and so, why not buy one of those facilities?

(While those of us who are steeped in eComm can get swept up in the idea that everything is moving online, Tim is absolutely right—approximately 85% of products are still bought in a store.)

B & P: What does this mean for brands, and what changes have you seen?

TS: Right after the purchase, there was lots of speculation about what would happen and when. Many of us thought Amazon [was] going to launch this thing, learn a little, and slowly make changes. Boy, was I proved wrong. As soon as the sale closed in August, it was clear Amazon had arrived when Echos (smart speakers that connect to a voice-controlled automated assistant) and lockers (a location for secure receipt of Amazon packages) started showing up in stores. Then there was the pivotal day when Prime Rewards launched nationwide. Suddenly, brokers who were long-valued partners with Whole Foods, participating in resets and other activities, were banned from stores. And the pay-to-play has become clearly defined and nonnegotiable.

(One of the big outstanding questions is how Amazon will scale what has been one of their most important initiatives, one fraught with challenges since its inception a decade ago: Amazon Fresh. Whether home delivery or click-and-collect, that last mile remains a challenge to all retailers except those with dedicated warehouses, and frankly a capability for home delivery that is the singular core of their business like FreshDirect, on the East Coast.)

B & P: What do you see in your crystal ball?

TS: Not much more immediate change, in terms of the customer experience. Amazon has quickly optimized that piece of the business. Amazon stands to make Whole Foods become more technologically savvy. And another dynamic yet to play itself out: how will Amazon work with the existing supply chain, where the largest natural distributor, UNFI (United Natural Foods, Inc.), is their primary product source, with Whole Foods representing approximately 30% of their overall business. It sounds like a negotiation yet to come.

One of the consequences of this purchase is the wake-up call it provided to other brick-and-mortar retailers that need to be smarter about eComm. In the long run, Tim believes it's also going to be good for smart independent retailers that are the antithesis of this trend toward big; a large group of consumers does not want to do business with any of the large behemoths.

And we agree, these are stores that will continue to thrive by differentiating themselves. This is really what all brick-and-mortar retailers—large and small—need to reflect on. Amazon buying Whole Foods is not a death knell. Tim likened this acquisition to what happened with independent book stores when Amazon first came on the scene. While the big book chains have struggled and some are now out of business, the store in his town just celebrated its forty-sixth anniversary. We've found this to be true in our towns as well.

Ironically, we think this new dynamic will actually be challenging for some of the new, small brands that are so successful on Amazon, as the ability to get an early foothold in stores by launching locally or regionally at Whole Foods has largely disappeared. What a strange dichotomy when you consider the ease that Amazon affords these very brands online.

Suffice it to say, there's more to come on the Amazon/Whole Foods front. But while we agree it may be one of the significant market disruptors of our time, it's not going to be the brand killer, nor will it mean the death of retail stores.

DO YOU NEED OTHER ECOMM PARTNERS?

Once your Amazon presence and sales start to show signs of life, you may begin considering other growth opportunities. Hopefully, you're cultivating direct relationships with customers on your own website to the greatest extent possible, since this creates the most value for your brand and business. And then you should expand into as many other third-party eComm platforms as possible, to further extend your online presence, right? Not necessarily.

This is another way the online world is different from brick and mortar. You don't need to continuously acquire new storefront placements to grow your business. In eComm, once you've achieved nationwide distribution, the challenge isn't placement, it's marketing.

Amazon owned about 44% of *all* eComm purchases in 2017 and is on track for nearly 49% in 2018; the next closest is eBay, at just under 7%. (And eBay isn't an appropriate market in the food space, for the most part.)

Based on our client experience, somewhere around 90%–95% of your online business will come from a combination of your website and Amazon, with *all* the other platforms combined making up the remainder. So allocate your time and business resources accordingly!

Notable runners-up include Thrive Market, which has the potential to be your next largest partner in the natural food space. Also, Vitacost is a long-established eComm retailer that may prove valuable for your business, and although it may not sound like it from their name, they offer a wide variety of products in food and beverage categories. Walmart, which purchased Jet.com's eComm expertise, is aggressively spending on capabilities and advertising, in a latecomer attempt to nip at Amazon's heels. Hopefully, this is not entirely futile, as competition is healthy for the marketplace. And if anyone has the resources and fulfillment prowess to compete with Amazon, it's Walmart.

WHAT ABOUT AMAZON INTERNATIONAL?

Amazon has multiple international platforms, currently 15 countries (4 of which are in the UK) in addition to the US. The next biggest opportunity is the UK, yet its sales volume is less than one-third that of the US. Because there is so much opportunity for sales volume in the US, we encourage our clients to take advantage of every last dollar on the table before considering expansion into other markets.

Since most small brands don't have the financial or staffing bandwidth to expand internationally, what seems like an easy next step is not really that simple. There's lots to consider—everything from tax implications to legitimate labeling to cultural differences that will impact the success of your product in a given market. As one of our New Zealand clients said, they had to learn how to speak "American" before they were able to provide effective content for their Amazon US product pages.

And then there's the unexpected. One of our clients went into Amazon UK at the very same time that Brexit was passed by voters. The economic and social uncertainty quickly created challenges to introducing new products to the UK market.

Regulations also contribute to each market being different and are often more complicated than you would expect. India, for example, enacted a policy restricting foreign multibrand retailers from selling directly to consumers online. So Amazon had to come up with creative way to harness the power of 3P sellers to create a business model that works.

Larger companies tend to have additional complexities to consider. Often a sales agent or broker is assigned to a particular country or region, so companies need to be sure they don't violate contractual obligations with these selling partners.

So if we haven't convinced you to keep your eye on the Amazon US prize, we implore you to at least do plenty of homework before you enter international territory.

15

———◦◦◦———

FINAL THOUGHTS

The world of eComm makes the word *dynamic* seem boring and meaningless. The rate of change online is simply dizzying. A decade ago, staying in tune with all the changes happening in eComm and digital marketing required full-time effort; today, it requires that effort simply to stay abreast of a *one or two eCommerce platforms or marketing channels*. As they have expanded in complexity and competitiveness, the knowledge base and experience required to remain an expert have increased in tandem.

Amazon is of course no exception, and in fact is in one of the fastest growth phases it has ever experienced. It has also begun to emerge as the fastest-growing advertising platform in existence, competing with the likes of Google and Facebook while simultaneously continuing to innovate in the areas of fulfillment and distribution. It is evolving into even more of a primary web property for brands and retailers to house their wares, competing with the brand's own website and other retailers.

Meanwhile, the worlds of grocery and natural food are being upended, in the beginning stages of a transformation that will unfold over the next decade with increasing rapidity. As the tumult that online connectivity has unleashed on retail at large finally begins to spread in earnest to the food space—everything is changing, from where we shop and order (moving online) to how we acquire the goods (moving to pick-up and even delivery)—there will be almost unimaginable change and innovation in the coming years. And of course massive opportunity, as the tightly controlled power of entrenched distribution begins to decentralize.

All of this we have discussed to some extent in the preceding pages. The point here is that any statements committed to writing about what IS in the digital world, and any resulting recommendations, have to be viewed through this lens with the understanding that current tactics will evolve or may become obsolete, often with frightening speed.

It is for this reason that we have tried to focus more on principles of success that will stand the test of time, rather than extremely specific points of execution that may literally change from day to day and even moment to moment.

The aforementioned rate of change is why we do what we do: help businesses thrive in the new environment. Your business will always require team members whose job it is to stay abreast of this rapid evolution, and at times you will benefit from outside guidance, expertise, or management. We find that some of our most successful clients return to work with us on specific issues or new developments, or to seek general guidance. Don't feel that you need to go it alone, as skilled resources can provide a trajectory for your business that would otherwise be unattainable. Reach out, use the experience of the masters, and take that increasingly traveled and successful route to market that others have paved for you. We wish you the best of luck in this exciting but sometimes complicated and always busy eCommerce landscape!

GLOSSARY

Term	Definition
3P or 3P Seller	Third-party seller that sells products on Amazon's site
A+ content/enhanced brand content	Detailed content on a product page, typically below the fold; great for loading search terms and brand storytelling
Amazon Family	Introduced as "Amazon Mom" in 2010, Amazon Family provides targeted products, messaging, and additional discounts. Members are both Prime and Subscribe and Save customers
Amazon Prime	Yearly membership program for two-day free shipping and other benefits like video streaming
Amazon Seller Central	Amazon's web-based seller portal for their third-party selling platform; used for completion of

new item paperwork, replenishing inventory, contracts, viewing brand metrics, forecasts, reports, filing cases, notifications as well as educational tools for selling on Amazon

Amazon Vendor Central — Amazon's web-based vendor portal for completion of new item paperwork, contracts, viewing brand metrics, forecasts, reports, and filing cases

AMG (Amazon Media Group) — Amazon's media/advertising division; works separately from Amazon but creates media programs that tie in with a brand's merchandising programs

Amazon Advertising — Formerly known as Amazon Marketing Services (AMS). A self-serve, pay-per-click advertising program on Vendor Central and Seller Central

ARA Premium — Amazon's premium vendor data package for sales and marketing consumer insights, typically costing 1% of sales and providing more detailed metrics

ASIN — Amazon Standard Identification Number (number assigned to each individual product)

Brand Registry	A program that enables some brand protection for product listing pages and access to certain additional programs. Requires a filed trademark and acceptance by Amazon
Consumables	Products in the Grocery, Body Care, Household, etc. spaces that are used and re-ordered on a regular basis.
CP	Contribution profit; metric for viewing profitability of product or brand; "margin" is obsolete concept in eCommerce
CPPU	Contribution profit per unit; metric for viewing profitability of product or brand; "margin" is obsolete concept in eCommerce
CRAP	Refers to an item that "can't realize a profit"
CRAPed -out	An item that "can't realize a profit" and has been discontinued
FBA	Fulfillment by Amazon; a model on the third-party seller platform where the seller lists the product and ships it into to Amazon FCs, yet still owns the product, while Amazon handles

	fulfillment and shipping to the consumer
FC	Fulfillment center
FFP	Frustration-Free Packaging; designed to minimize packaging and waste, yet still provide protection for the shipped items
HOTW (Hands off the Wheel)	Amazon philosophy of their involvement with vendor and seller businesses; designed to use Amazon's automated portals
Lightning Deal	A product promotion for a brief period, for typically 4 hours with a very aggressive discount
Obso	Short for Obsolete - An item that has been turned off for sale or discontinued; this can sometimes be an error in their system, so it's important to follow up
PCOGS	Purchased cost of goods; the cost of goods to Amazon of product purchased on "Vendor Central"
PDP	Product detail page; specific product page for a given ASIN
Planned Replenishment	Status for an item that is live on-site and being ordered regularly

PPC	Advertising term that refers to pay-per-click
Prime Now	A program for Prime members offering select household items and essentials with ultrafast delivery
Prime Pantry	A program for Prime members that packages nonperishable grocery items to deliver in single box for a flat fee
ROAS	Return on ad spend; metric for advertising expenditure; a ratio of revenue to ad spend
SIOC	Ships in own container; a product package that enables the product to be shipped in its original packaging
Sponsored Brands	Previously called Headline Search Ads; ad format displaying above all other search results; requires completed Brand Registry
Sponsored Products	Amazon's core pay-per-click advertising program
Storefront	Your brand's website on Amazon; requires completed Brand Registry
Subscribe & Save (S&S)	Amazon's consumables subscription program

Vine	Amazon's item sample program available on the Vendor Central platform; provides samples to a qualified group of reputable reviewers on Amazon, who then review the products on the site
VPC	Amazon Vendor Power Coupon; lives on the product page and prompts buyer to click to use

ABOUT THE AUTHORS

Betsy McGinn
CEO of McGinn eComm
As Seventh Generation's first eCommerce channel director, Betsy pioneered the company's innovative eComm strategy and created a thriving multimillion-dollar partnership with Amazon.

Since founding McGinn eComm in 2014, Betsy has worked with hundreds of natural products brands to successfully launch, optimize, and recalibrate their Amazon business. From product development and profitability analysis to alignment of their multifunctional teams, McGinn eComm guides clients through every step of this complex channel, helping to ensure successful and profitable online businesses.

With more than a decade of eCommerce experience, Betsy is a thought-leader and regular speaker at workshops and conferences globally.

Visit Betsy at mcginnecomm.com

Philip Segal
Founder of Digital Native Marketing
As the digital strategist behind nutpods' wildly successful online presence, Phil began his career in digital marketing with an SEO internship in 2006 after a change of heart about law school. This experience led to several more opportunities to manage digital channels for a wide variety of small businesses and national brands. With special expertise in executing media campaigns—from platform minimums to over $1 million per month—Phil has years of experience in hands-on management and achieving aggressive growth for his clients while working with top talent across the digital space.
Visit Phil at DigitalNative.co (not .com!)

Made in the USA
Middletown, DE
23 May 2020